Enza Lyons

ADD / ADHD
BREAKTHROUGH

How to increase concentration, focused attention, build self-esteem and achieve success at school and in life

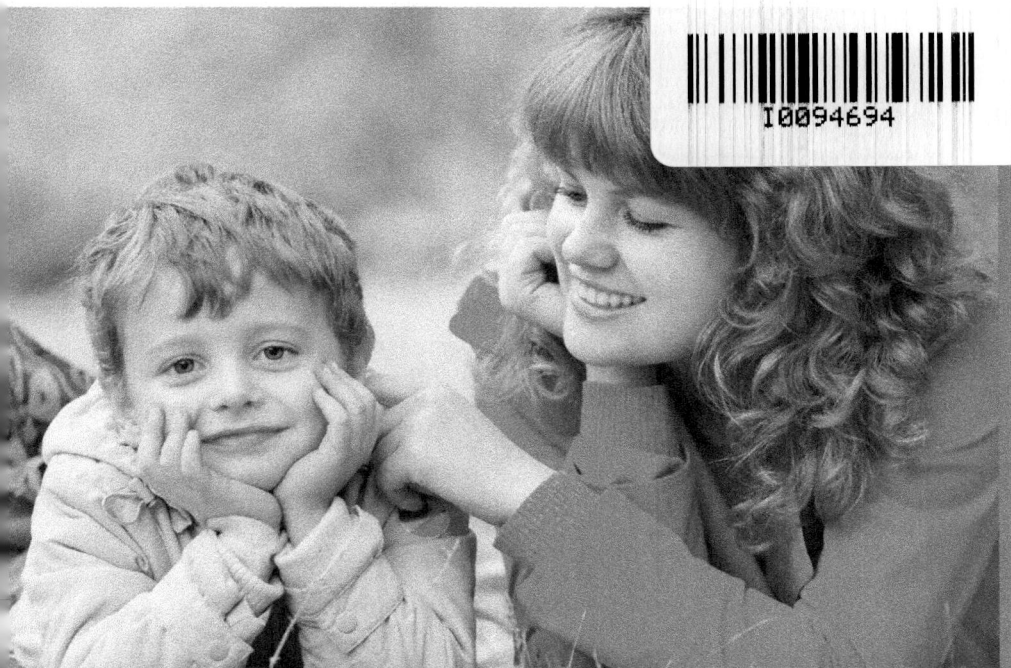

Parent Guide

Parent Guide
ADD / ADHD Breakthrough
How to increase concentration, focused attention,
build self-esteem and achieve success at school
and in life by Enza Lyons

Enza Lyons
P.O. Box 601,
North Lakes Qld 4509 Australia
https://calendly.com/enzalyons
Phone: 0413 697 692
Published by Enza Lyons
Brisbane, Queensland, Australia
Cover designed by Ngirl Design

Catalogue-in-Publications details available on request from the Australian
National Library

ISBN: 978-0-9873415-1-8

The information contained in this book is for educational purposes only, in
believing that readers will become more informed on the choices that are
available to parents to help their loved ones overcome ADD / ADHD naturally
and with success.

Medical Disclaimer

The information contained herein is not intended to diagnose, treat, cure
or prevent any disease, nor should it be used as a substitute for your own
physician's advice. The author recommends that you do your own research
and consult a qualified medical health professional before choosing to
pursue a medical treatment plan. Before beginning any exercise program,
it is advisable to check with your professional healthcare practitioner. The
information is for educational purposes only in believing that readers will
become more informed on the choices that are available. I encourage you to
become an educated person because ultimately the choices made, are up to
you and that you take full responsibility for your decisions. Every effort has
been made to ensure that the information presented in this book is accurate.

Brain Gym® is a registered trademark of Brain Gym® International/Educational
Kinesiology Foundation

Dedication
To parents and educators

Praises for ADD / ADHD Breakthrough

Reading Enza's Parent Guide, ADD / ADHD Breakthrough was fantastic because it filled a lot of gaps in my knowledge and has enabled me to make better choices about my children's health. I was also ecstatic to find such practical advice on how to improve my children's reading, writing, concentration and general well-being – all through natural, drug-free remedies.

Seeing my two sons struggle in the classroom was heartbreaking. I felt powerless to help them. As any parent would, I sought advice and support from teachers, physicians and family members – anything to help my boys! After taking my sons for private sessions with Enza, I've seen dramatic improvements with both my sons after only two sessions. I know these techniques work because my beautiful boys are now more confident, have higher self- esteem, and have improved their writing, reading and coordination. I highly recommend this book to parents of children with ADHD and hyperactivity – I'll be keeping it on hand to refer to it frequently. Thanks, Enza."

Amy, Mother

"Over the years, I have seen Enza's passion for drugless rehabilitation of ADD, ADHD students result in research and constant updating of her training. In her clinic, the success stories are very impressive. I welcome her publication of her book as it enables the caring parents of ADD, ADHD children to have easy access to the latest research. The organization of Enza's book makes topics so easy to find. As a mother, Enza knows how to convey information to other parents simply and directly. It is so easy to understand.

Her attention to detail is impressive and indicative of her dedication to sharing her information with anyone who seeks it. As a teacher who deals with anxious parents and concerned teachers daily, I well be recommending her book every chance I get because I have never been happy with the drug focus in dealing with ADD / ADHD. The side effects worry me. Now parents can be armed with very important substantiated facts that I am sure will assist them to make better choices for their loved ones."

Sandra Petersen, B.Ed.A.P.D., Dip. Cl.H., Teacher

"I have recently read Enza's book on ADD / ADHD Breakthrough. I am a Early Childhood teacher and a parent who has a son who has been a client of Enza's. I found the book an easy read with straight forward language. I was interested in all the background information about ADHD including the chapter on diet. It has a lot of practical ideas and has given me a further understanding of ADHD. This book is a valuable resource for both parents and teachers and I highly recommend it."

Alison, Early childhood teacher and mother

Table of contents

Special Acknowledgements

Thank you to the numerous people who I have come across in life who have helped shape my life, the writing of my books, philosophy and understanding of my work in child and brain development in order to assist children and adults achieve their goals and accomplish more in life. I am grateful to my clients who have taught me so much and who have allowed me to share their wonderful success stories. They have shown me the wonderful miraculous ability of the mind and body to heal. I am so grateful to the creator who created life, the incredible universe and the great purpose for all of mankind.

Thank you to the numerous researchers, educators and therapists whose work has contributed enormously to my own personal growth and maturity, my own work with children and adults. In particular to Dr. Paul Dennison Ph.D and Gail Dennison developing Brain Gym®, Carla Hannaford Ph.D., Physiology of the Brain, Carol Ann Erickson, Movement Development, Gorden Stokes and Daniel Whiteside, Three in One Concepts, Anna McRobert, Trevor Savage, Ann Summers, Wayne Topping Ph.D, Dr Harald Blomberg M.D. and Moira Dempsy, for Rhythmic Movement Training and many others. Thank you for your books, workshops and encouragement through my quest in understanding about the brain, the mind, the body, the importance of movement and the ability for the body to heal from emotional stress and trauma. Thank you to my friends and many others who have supported me through this journey.

Thank you, especially to my family who have really made the difference in my life. To my husband, my closest friend Keith, for his unending support, encouragement and love. To my parents who have given me love and support. To my children and grandchildren, who are the joys and fun of my life and who have taught me so much about unconditional love.

Learning about the joys of raising the next generation is a privilege and a blessing. Being a parent and grandparent is both challenging and rewarding, frustrating and joyous. It is the most fulfilling job a person can do. I enjoy assisting other people enrich their lives.

PREFACE

A whole new world awaits you

Remember when school teaching used to be an enjoyable and fulfilling career as one made a difference in the lives of the young? In many parts of the Western world that is no longer the case! The epidemic increase of ADHD (Attention Deficit Hyperactive Disorder), ADD (Attention Deficit Disorder), dyslexia and other learning disabilities, and the more recent rapid increase in students with autism and Asperger's syndrome have meant much more disruption in the classroom and a need to focus on those students who are learning-challenged, usually to the detriment of the remaining students.

Parents of such children are often at their wit's end. Frustrated by their child's behaviours and learning challenges within the classroom and behavioural problems at home the parents feel trapped. They desperately want positive changes for their child but they are at a loss as to what they can do. And the home front often becomes a battle ground filled with lots of tension. Some parents feel guilty as if they are genetically at fault, or feel out of control, lacking the parenting skills to handle a challenging situation. It is quite frustrating for teachers, parents and the children.

The medical profession has offered its solution – central nervous system stimulants such as Ritalin and Concerta. It is estimated that 7-10 % of American children, mainly boys, are being treated with central nervous system stimulants. True, such children are calmer in school. However, there are considerable hidden costs. When children go on a "Ritalin vacation" during the summer the side effects include depression and suicidal tendency. Researchers have discovered that users of CNS stimulants have increased aggressive and antisocial behaviour, and increased risk for later use of cigarettes, cocaine and other stimulants. And several research studies have shown no improvement in academic performance.

In the past, out of desperation, many parents have allowed their child to be put onto CNS stimulants. Increasingly we now see parents looking for drugless alternatives.

What is causing this tremendous increase in cases of ADHD and ADD? I remember reading of research done through Australian National University at the time when television first became available. Hyperactivity was absent among the rural children who weren't exposed to television but was present among the urban children who watched television. TV means exposure to increased electromagnetic frequencies, violence on TV, longer evenings, less sleep, and less burning off energy running around outside. These are life style changes which have become intensified as our Western societies have developed. Instead of natural play outside, many children now spend their time cooped up inside playing video games, texting, tweeting, etc. They are now sedentary, gaining weight, and spending a lot of time at a fixed focal distance. This is not healthy for a developing brain.

Over the past few decades the family structure has broken down. Many kids are now in one-parent homes living with a parent that is working. Over-worked parents don't have as much time to spend with their children and cannot always provide the structure children need for security. Lack of sufficient exercise, inadequate sleep, stressed out, and often going to school with no breakfast or a highly-refined carbohydrate-rich breakfast is not a good formula for learning within the classroom environment. No wonder that we as a society are reaping the whirlwind!

General deterioration in the food supply with its artificial colourings and flavourings, artificial sweeteners, MSG, and highly refined grains means that most people in our Western cultures are deficient in essential nutrients, craving junk foods, getting fatter, and becoming more sluggish, etc. Combine that with our use of play pens and walkers for children in our developed world which ensures even less movement. Movement is the key to wiring up the brain and, therefore, learning. No wonder we are in a crisis!

The medical profession cannot identify the cause for ADHD and ADD. This is probably because there is no single cause. Rather it is a perfect storm of a number of factors that I have already described: increased electromagnetic pollution, environmental toxins such as lead, inadequate nutrition, breakdown of the family, poor parenting skills and lack of movement.

All is not lost, however. Innovative developments since the 1960s can now offer us drug-free alternatives for conditions such as ADHD and ADD. One of these is specialised kinesiology where muscle monitoring is a biofeedback tool identifying areas of emotional stress, environmental stressors, foods to which the individual is sensitive and learning challenges. After acupressure points are massaged or other reflexes held or rubbed the muscle can again be monitored. A locked response tells us that we have been successful, an unlocked response that we need to further balancing. These results are immediate and usually noticed by both client and practitioner.

Brain Gym® / Educational Kinesiology has a particular focus on addressing people with learning challenges. For example, have a child or adult read out aloud. A trained consultant may notice their difficulty with horizontal tracking of the eyes, or poor quality in the voice; maybe the person tells the consultant that they fall asleep easily when they read. Massaging two specific acupressure points for about 30 seconds usually results in significant improvement in eye tracking ability, tone of reading voice, and now the person stays awake while reading. Maybe they have difficulty recalling what they read. Three different Brain Gym® activities can be switched on to improve that aspect of brain function. It almost sounds magical to get such dramatic shifts that quickly. This is why I gave up being a geology professor to embark on a new career as a kinesiologist 32 years ago! Such Brain Gym® activities are simple, yet very effective and can be used at home to reinforce the effects.

Rhythmic Movement Training is a totally different approach that Enza Lyons has available for her students and clients. Early in life we have primitive reflexes that are responsible for our survival and early development. As our brain and nervous system develop, these reflexes should become extinguished and give way to postural reflexes that guide our more mature automatic movements. However, in cases of ADHD and ADD some of these primitive reflexes are still in existence. Specific rhythmic movements can be used to extinguish those reflexes and integrate the individual so that they can function at a higher level. This generally alleviates symptoms such as those of ADHD and ADD.

In grade 1 Enza's son was experiencing significant learning challenges. The school didn't have any solutions. Enza was frustrated. However, she did find the answers in the relatively new fields of kinesiology and Brain Gym®. For more than two decades Enza has passionately pursued those interests and applied herself diligently to helping as many people as possible who have been frustrated by their own learning challenges or those of their children.

Using kinesiology and noticing how clients perform specific activities or movements, allows a consultant such as Enza to come up with an individualised program to help resolve learning difficulties, and to determine which foods or substances many be having a detrimental effect on the body, etc. It is quite beyond the scope of this book to detail all of this information. However, what Enza has done, very admirably, is to let you know that there is hope. Most people with ADHD and ADD can be helped with a drug-free approach.

Frustrated parents and teachers can be well-intentioned yet criticise the learning-challenged child. That additional stress likely results in worse performance, not better. One of the most valuable aspects of this book is an expansive description of communication skills that will create the structure that people with ADHD and ADD need. This information alone is well worth the cost of this book. You are not alone! Others have gone before you. You can benefit from what they have found works for them.

As a kinesiologist who has taught in 23 countries and trained in many disciplines including Brain Gym® and Rhythmic Movement Training I can assure you: it works.

Welcome to a whole new world where I am sure you will find the answers you are seeking.

Wayne W. Topping, Ph.D.
Founder of Wellness Kinesiology,
Author, educator.

About the author—Why I wrote this book

Hi, For over 20 years in my private practice, I have assisted many children and adults struggling with reading, writing, math, concentration and with early learning difficulties including ADD, ADHD, Dyspraxia, Dyslexia, delayed development and others. The results in my clients have been amazing using educational programs such as Kinesiology, Brain Gym® and Rhythmic Movement Training combined as a safe, natural therapy that has transformed lives.

My interest in using natural therapies to achieve optimal health and performance started very early in life. At the age of 18, I was experiencing a number of health problems, including severe acne. After studying everything I could on nutrition, exercise and other natural health principles I was able to implement a program that cleared my acne, radically improved my general health and boosted my energy.

Many years later I was married and after the birth of my second child I began suffering from lingering lower back pain. After receiving only temporary relief from chiropractic treatments, I visited a Kinesiology practitioner and was astonished by the immediate results. I wanted to know more about this amazing science.

Life was busy managing a family business and raising two children. Then I began to receive letters that my son was having trouble learning in grade 1. He couldn't settle down to lessons and was being put outside of the classroom. He did not want to go to school anymore. He was 'assessed' but no-one was able to offer any practical advice in those days. I was upset and feeling helpless. I couldn't understand why such a bright child was having these problems.

Fortunately, I discovered Kinesiology and Brain Gym®. In the natural health field, Kinesiology uses movement and muscle testing to detect and release imbalances or stresses in the body. Brain Gym® is part of Educational Kinesiology – an educational program using movement to increase the physical skills of daily life activities and promoting the joy of learning for more efficient learning and quality of life. In 1986, I remember how I felt when I completed my first workshop taught by Dr Paul and Gail Dennison in Educational Kinesiology in-depth course, which Brain Gym® is a part of, I felt terrific, no more sore muscles and free to move in my body. I have gained so much from doing the workshops while learning how to help my children. It has given me a simple effective tool to reduce anxiety, release tense muscles, improve learning, comprehension, organization, coordination and much more.

At the time, I was very excited to discover these safe and natural ways to help my son, but the teachers weren't interested. So began my journey to learn everything I could about the brain, learning, Kinesiology and Brain Gym®. Many think that Brain Gym® is only for children to help them develop all kinds of academic, coordination and intrapersonal skills. The secret is out and adults are using Brain Gym® movements to help themselves. Workers are more focused and productive in the workplace. Athletes and musicians are better coordinated and mentally ready to perform at their peak. Parents are able to reduce stress levels, improve their child's behaviour and bring harmony into the home.

For over 26 years I have helped myself, my family, friends and thousands of clients, including children.

In my private practice, I have used safe, natural therapies such as Kinesiology, Brain Gym® and Rhythmic Movement Training, to produce amazing results that have transformed lives. For example, I will use kinesiology techniques to determine whether the body is absorbing its nutrients optimally. Nutrition plays a major role in determining how we look and feel. It is reflected in the quality of our skin and how well our bodies function. Adrenal and emotional stress may interfere with the ability of the body to absorb maximum nutrition leading to impaired body function. Releasing meridian energy blockages can greatly improve the body's ability to absorb maximum nutrition.

Rhythmic Movement Training (RMT) is a recent addition to my education and research. Combining this with Brain Gym® has transformed the lives of many of my clients. RMT is a 'new', drug-free approach to dramatically improve learning and overcome emotional and behavioural challenges. It looks at the role of developmental movements that babies make naturally. There movements are crucial for laying down the foundations for the neural network, pathway growth, and myelinisation within the brain, to assist our learning as we grow and develop, and our transitioning to the lifelong postural reflexes..

In recent years I have been talking to numerous teachers and parents. I am saddened to hear about the increase in learning difficulties, behavioural problems, the low self-esteem, poor self image of children and the increase of depression in teenagers. Parents feeling helpless and not knowing where to go. More people need to know that there are safe, natural ways to overcome ADD and ADHD safely, naturally and without drugs. I would like to encourage parents to be proactive to turn their families into a happy, calm and harmonious family. It is possible!

Here's what one teacher has to say....

> **Brain Gym® Is A Simple Yet Powerful Tool That Has Transformed My Classroom**
>
> *"In over twenty years of teaching infants/primary school children one of the most amazing 'tools' I have used in my classroom has been Brain Gym® exercises.*
>
> *In my class of children aged five to seven, many students were unsettled, stressed and angry. Consequently, many were experiencing learning difficulties and displaying very challenging and disruptive behaviour.*
>
> *After introducing daily Brain Gym® exercises, the results have been amazing. Many of the parents have commented how their children are progressing in many different areas including coordination, balance and confidence. Parents are telling me that their children are much happier and will even do the Brain Gym® exercises at home to help themselves to relax and cope with challenging situations.*
>
> *One particular grade two student was experiencing difficulties with her reading and writing, was putting a lot of pressure on herself, was often very tired and was finding it difficult to relax. After three or four sessions with Enza, this student's reading and writing improved greatly and she has greater confidence in herself. She has transformed from a little girl who was often upset by the 'smallest things', to a happy child who is so much more energetic and confident in herself and her abilities.*
>
> *Brain Gym® is a simple but very powerful 'tool' and it can really make a difference in children's lives. I would highly recommend it to other teachers and parents."* Sandra Williams, School teacher

Of course, every parent must decide for themselves what is best for their child. I trust you find this book helpful in making those decisions. Becoming more informed will assist you in making better choices. It's a step towards a better life for you, your child, and everyone around you! You can put an end to ADD and ADHD naturally and effectively!

I have written this book to share my knowledge and to make parents aware of the options they have to help their ADD / ADHD diagnosed child overcome the disorder and live a very successful life.

I trust that by providing the information in this book, no parent need feel as helpless as I did all those years ago. You now have the power to help your ADHD child naturally, safely and without drugs.

I wish you and your family vibrant health, mental clarity and radiant well-being. You deserve it!

Enza Lyons
Licensed Brain Gym® Instructor/Consultant (Brain Gym® International/Educational Kinesiology Foundation)
Registered Kinesiology Practitioner (Member of A.K.A., A.T.M.S.)
Rhythmic Movement Training Consultant
Brisbane, Australia
https://calendly.com/enzalyons
Phone: 0413 697 692

CHAPTER 1

What choices do I have to help my ADHD child?

Many of you who are reading this today, are parents or grandparents and you may not remember any children in your school classes being diagnosed with Attention Deficit Disorder (ADD) or Attention Deficit Hyperactivity Disorder (ADHD), or being medicated during school days. Indeed, just a few decades ago, these terms were rarely heard of.

Surely, there have always been "problem children" that did not conform to the standards that teachers and parents would like. These were the kids that made the teacher's job a challenge: they did not pay attention or were the class clowns, always disrupting. Frequently disorganised and behind in their schoolwork, they often received lots of extra, though negative, attention from the teachers and principal at school, and ultimately their parents.

Sound familiar at all?

In the recent past, ADD and ADHD diagnoses have skyrocketed. Most people know children that take ADD medications of one kind or another, and it is now the most common ailment affecting school age children. Additionally, adults in large numbers are asking for and receiving testing and eventually medication for ADD. Even with all the pharmaceuticals dispensed, most people really do not know much about ADD or ADHD, or understand how it affects a person.

It's not to say that ADD or ADHD do not exist; indeed they do, and left untreated it can seriously impair the dynamics of families, classrooms, and other group settings when the afflicted person is present. It can be emotionally draining, stressful, and overall, simply maddening!

Aside from the daily aggravation, there are serious social repercussions when ADD or ADHD are left unchecked. Children with ADD/ADHD often have low self-esteem that causes them problems in school and later life. When they are experiencing learning challenges at school, as teens they will tend to skip school regularly, are much more likely to use drugs or alcohol and not complete high school.

Obviously, there are plenty of reasons for parents to be concerned and want to help "cure" their children of ADHD. Frequently, the first advice given by well-meaning medical practitioners is to medicate them with psychostimulant drugs such as ADHD drugs such as Ritalin and Adderall.

Luckily, more studies are giving us facts about serious side effects of these drugs, in both the short and long term. In this book, I will explain those findings and offer alternative treatments and natural remedies that parents can utilize to aid their children safely without the use of heavy medications.

Good news

I have good news for parents about ADHD. I have prepared this book to help parents become more informed and make better choices for their ADHD diagnosed child.

Brain Gym® is an educational program that encourages sensory motor development for easier and more efficient learning. As a learning and behaviour specialist in child development and licensed Brain Gym® teacher, I have assisted children struggling with early learning difficulties including ADD, ADHD, Dyslexia and other similar conditions. With this safe, drug-free, natural solution, children have been able to improve their concentration, listening and comprehension, physical coordination, speech, reasoning and creativity, confidence and self esteem, social interaction and general well-being.

This is certainly what happened with Jack. This is how Jack got his life back from out of control to being happier and more successful at school and sports.

These natural treatments have been shown to optimise brain development to produce increased focus and better learning – without harmful physical side-effects.

Some of the key natural, drug-free solutions discussed in this book are Brain Gym® and Rhythmic Movement Training. These programs help children improve their concentration, listening and comprehension, physical co-ordination, speech, reasoning and creativity, confidence and self esteem, social interaction and general well-being. They also encourage sensory motor development.

In addition to this sensory motor development program, this book will explain the role of nutrition in helping children overcome ADHD – and the 'brain power' foods every child should be eating. We'll also be discussing all the other issues that accompany a diagnosis of ADHD, such as dealing with anger and frustration, coping with stress in the family, modifying behaviour, and creating productive classroom learning opportunities. We'll identify certain behaviours that you can change and help you figure out ways to minimise this disorder in your life so you and your family can live more normally than ever before!

Next, we'll learn more about ADHD drugs and alternative remedies.

This is how Jack went from a life that was out of control to a life with increased happiness and success in school and sports.

I met Jack when he was 12 years old and he had been taking medication since he was four years old for ADHD (Attention Deficit Hyperactivity Disorder). He struggled with inattention, hyperactivity and impulsivity. His mother wanted to take him off the medication, but was afraid of what might happen with his erratic behaviour.

I taught Jack Brain Gym® exercises to help him take charge of his emotions and become more cooperative.

Incredibly, by our third session, his mother was able to take him off the ADHD drugs he had been on for eight years. With Brain Gym®, Jack was able to control his behaviour and feel more relaxed and energetic. And more importantly, he was able to handle responsibilities with maturity. Once his brain and body began working together, many areas of Jack's life improved including his reading, writing, coordination, breathing, communication and ultimately, his confidence. He has been achieving As for all his school subjects.

CHAPTER 2

ADHD drugs and alternative remedies

The drugs commonly used to treat ADHD are known as psychostimulants. They inlcude Ritalin (methylphenidate), Dexedrine (dextroamphetamine), Cyleit (pemoline) and Adderall (amphetamine). These drugs work by increasing the levels of certain chemicals in the brain, also called neurotransmitters, which help transmit signals between nerves.

This action does slow down the brain to enable children to focus on repetitive, detailed schoolwork. However, it also impacts the brain in other ways. The drugs decrease and/or inhibit the function of natural, self-produced neurotransmitters. As a result, children are less able to activate whole-brain thinking. They have difficulty shifting focus from the details to the big picture, which is so vital to creative problem-solving. In addition, psychostimulants can reduce children's innate motivation to seek out new experiences, to play and to learn.

> **"Ritalin is one of the drugs used for treating Hyperactivity and Attention Deficit Disorders...**
>
> *Ritalin acts on the brain just like "speed" – neuropharmacologically it has the same effects, side effects and risks as cocaine and amphetamines. The FDA classifies Ritalin in the high addiction category, Schedule 11, with amphetamines, cocaine, morphine, opium and barbiturates."* Treatments of Psychiatric Disorders, A Task Force Report of the American Psychiatric Association, Washington, DC APA, 1989. p.1221

The ADHD drugs temporarily treat the symptoms of ADHD. They do nothing when it comes to addressing ADD and ADHD's root cause and have no long term beneficial effect.

Some of the documented side-effects of these drugs include:

> ➤ Decreased appetite/weight loss

> ➤ Insomnia

> ➤ Headaches

> ➤ Nervousness

> ➤ Social withdrawal

> ➤ Stomach aches

> ➤ Heart palpitations

In view of the potentially detrimental short and long-term effects of drug use, it is not surprising that many parents are now questioning the use of drugs as the first choice for ADHD treatment.

In fact, there are alternative therapies which have been shown to assist in brain development to produce increased focus and improved learning – without harmful physical side-effects.

> *"When the research so strongly shows that integrated movement, supportive touch, music and play grow brain areas necessary for increased focus and learning for a lifetime, without detrimental physical effects, why do we use potentially harmful drugs as a first resort?"* Carla Hannaford, *"Smart Moves"*

In particular, Brain Gym® and Rhythmic Movement Training are simple, natural, drug-free solutions. Brain Gym® is a simple yet powerful learning program that enable children to increase brain function for improved concentration, listening and comprehension, physical coordination, speech, reasoning and creativity, confidence and self esteem, social interaction and general well-being.

The basis of the therapy is movement. Scientific research has shown that, from birth, movement is vital to brain development and the learning process. Each new movement encourages new neural connections – super highways for intellectual and physical growth. And the recent discovery of neuroplasticity has proven that new nerve cells and neural connections can be formed throughout life – regardless of age.

Thus, Brain Gym® can be used by children and adults to stimulate better neural   connections and improve brain   performance. These simple, fun exercises and techniques will benefit anyone, but especially those with learning or attention disorders such as ADD or ADHD.

> In her book *"Smart Moves"* Carla Hannaford PhD explains: *"Brain Gym® facilitates each step of the [learning] process by waking up the mind/body system and bringing it to learning readiness."*

Before introducing a potentially harmful drug to a child's system, it seems sensible to first ensure they have been given the opportunity to develop their natural body-brain connection and innate potential for healing and learning. This alone, achieved through therapies such as Brain Gym® and other motor sensory integration programs, can produce amazing transformations in children diagnosed with ADD and ADHD.

Next, we'll learn more about the condition itself.

CHAPTER 3

A different way of looking at ADHD

Attention Deficit Hyperactivity Disorder (ADHD) or Attention Deficit Disorder (ADD) as commonly called, are neurological (nervous system) disorder, often present from a young age that manifests themselves in a number of ways. They can include easy distractibility, forgetfulness, hyperactivity, and poor control of impulses.

Children that are easily distracted, inattentive, become bored easily with what they are currently doing, have problems organising their tasks, or controlling their impulses are usually quickly labeled as ADHD. If they have problems with attention, but no hyperactivity, then the condition is typically called ADD. In fact, children that have hunched posture and lack of muscle tone are more prone to developing ADD. Such children often swing between hyperactivity and passivity, with the hyperactive portion being a way to stimulate their brain. In extreme cases, children that have very low muscle tone that get much less exercise from movement also get less stimulation, so they tend to daydream instead of having periods of hyperactivity.

ADHD is considered a chronic syndrome — which means it cannot be cured, though it can be controlled and the effects can be minimised. Experts say that three to five percent of the United States population, both adults and children, are believed to be affected by the disorder.

There is a lot of controversy about ADHD diagnosis, including whether being diagnosed with ADHD is a true disability. Some doctors and other medical personnel believe the condition is psychological in nature, and there is continuing debate over ADHD treatment among medical personnel around the world. Some doctors support behaviour modification and sensory movement programs, while others believe that only medication offers relief.

The generally accepted method of treatment has traditionally been medication, though that is quite upsetting to parents of small children, who are being diagnosed as young as three or four years of age. Medication of pre-school children causes some critical parents, educators, and anti-medication clinicians to become extremely outspoken about the potential dangers of medicating our children.

Other scientists and medical personnel believe that people with this condition have a delayed maturity process within their brains; the child has not been significantly stimulated through all of its senses and the nerve system has not completely woven itself together well, as it does with the majority of people.

We can study small children and consider a different angle altogether; children of around twelve months of age that are given "free rein" and are allowed to freely move around exhibit behaviour that is quite similar to that of older children with ADD or ADHD. Note that children who are made to sit in a baby walker, swing, high chair, or car seat are often unhappy little people, and want to get out and explore their surroundings. Those one year olds that are allowed to freely play have some similarities:

➤ They are constantly moving, climbing, and exploring.

➤ They typically do not pay attention to adult instruction.

> ➢ They have trouble deciding what to do first, and then next.

> ➢ They are easily distracted.

> ➢ They do not control impulses well.

The majority of these children, without help or medication, outgrow their hyperactivity and attention disorder, as they get older.

Why are some children different? Why don't they all overcome their attention challenges as they age? What specific part of their makeup is unknown to the experts and causes some children to remain hyperactive and unable to concentrate? These questions remain unanswered.

The baby's brain certainly has not matured. For proper brain functioning, all of a person's neural connections must develop. Properly developed nerve fibres are coated with insulating myelin, and the foundation for this growth is critical throughout the first years of life. In fact, estimates are that newborn babies develop 4.7 million nerve cell branches in their brain every single minute of the first year of life.

This process is highly dependent on outside stimulation of all the infant's senses to develop adequately. Especially crucial during this period is stimulation of the tactile, balance, and kinaesthetic senses. A baby gets these stimulations by being touched and rocking, and by making continuous rhythmic movements of his own. Most babies follow a similar pattern of development—turning over, rolling, creeping along on their stomachs, rocking on their hands and knees, and then crawling are all important parts of normal development. All of these things taken together stimulate the baby's brain during the first year, and they are the foundation for all future development, and the maturation of the child's brain.

Children without adequate stimulation of these types can have delays in brain maturity or obvious impairments. This delayed development can manifest itself as attention disorder, with or without the related hyperactivity. When babies are unable, or not permitted, to move around sufficiently, they get insufficient stimulation of the neocortex and frontal lobes of the brain. Indications typically show up as sluggishness, hypoactivity, inattention, and late developing.

Many of the children diagnosed with ADHD have poor muscle tone and often a hunched posture. This poor posture causes shallow breathing and not enough oxygen to reach and stimulate the brain, especially the neo-cortex. These children might swing wildly between periods of extreme hyperactivity and lethargy, with the active periods stimulating to the brain.

ADHD is defined by the American Academy of Pediatrics (AAP) as a brain condition that makes it hard for children to control their behaviour; diagnosis is complicated because there is no precise test for the condition. The disorder can cause children difficulty with interpersonal relationships, trouble in school, both academically and behaviour-wise, and poor self-esteem.

How do you recognize ADHD? Children with ADHD cannot control their responses to their environment. This lack of control makes them inattentive, hyperactive and impulsive.

The symptoms fall into three categories.

The first category is inattention. Symptoms include:

> Trouble keeping attention focused during play or tasks

➤ Often does not pay close attention to details or makes careless mistakes when doing schoolwork or other activities

➤ Appearing not to listen when spoken to

➤ Failing to follow instructions or finish schoolwork, chores and tasks

➤ Avoiding tasks that require a high amount of mental effort and organisation such as school projects

➤ Frequently losing items required to facilitate tasks or activities such as school supplies

➤ Excessive distractibility

➤ Forgetfulness

➤ Procrastination or inability to begin an activity

The second is Hyperactivity Behaviour. Symptoms include:

➤ Fidgeting with hands or feet

➤ Squirming in a seat

➤ Leaving a seat often even at inappropriate times as if driven by a motor

➤ Running or climbing at inappropriate times

➤ Difficulty during quiet play

➤ Frequently feeling restless

➤ Excessive talking

The third is Impulsive Behaviour – Symptoms include:

➤ Interrupting the activities of others at inappropriate times.

➤ Answering a question before the speaker has finished

➤ Failing to wait for one's turn

A positive diagnosis usually comes after the child or person exhibits at least six of the above symptoms for three months or more. Symptoms will usually be consistent, regardless of the environment—they are similar whether at home, school, or somewhere else, and they interfere with "normal" functioning.

People that are inattentive often find focusing on a task difficult and they get easily bored. While doing things they enjoy, on the other hand, they might exhibit natural concentration, while learning something new or organizing and completing simple tasks prove difficult at times.

Those people with hyperactivity exude boundless energy; they seem to literally bounce off the walls and cannot stay still even for short periods. Impulsive people do not think first; they simply act or speak without considering the consequences. They also have a hard time waiting for anything; everything must happen right now.

Of course, almost everyone reading this can identify themselves in the behaviours I have just outlined. We can all be hyperactive, impulsive, or inattentive at times; that does not mean we have

ADHD. The behaviours are only symptoms of the disorder in young children, seven or younger. However, ADHD and the age of onset can vary, and symptoms might not even appear until the teen years.

Symptoms must be pervasive and continual, and occur more frequently than other people in the same age range. Behaviour that causes a real disability in two or more areas of a person's life—school, social interactions, work, or family can signal ADHD or ADD.

Males are diagnosed with ADHD three times more often, causing some doctors to call for gender specific testing since the symptoms present themselves differently in boys versus girls, accounting for the statistical differences.

Children with ADHD frequently engage in disruptive activities and antisocial behaviour that alienates their peers and others; their school performance typically suffers due to their easy distractibility and inability to focus.

It can be extremely stressful for the parents of a child with ADHD; frustrations run high when they attempt to discipline them. Marital problems and even divorce result from some of the worst cases.

ADHD can last into adulthood. The good news is that symptoms can be alleviated with the strategies in this book.

The good news about ADHD is that recent years have seen an increase in the overall understanding of what the disorder looks like. We know that not every child with ADHD is hyperactive, and not every child who is inattentive has ADHD. Many children have been wrongly misdiagnosed.

Brain Gym® and Rhythmic Movement Training have been found to be effective and successful programs in assisting children and adults with ADD / ADHD. The movements and techniques replicate the rhythmic movements an infant naturally makes in order to stimulate the brain to build better foundation. This is great news. They provide sensory stimulation to develop nerve nets of the brain stem, cerebellum, basal ganglia and neo-cortex; improve attention and concentration; decrease hyperactivity and impulsivity. Because it increases muscle tone, the child improves in body posture, breathing and endurance.

Through much research by neuroscientists, they have discovered that the brain can change. Best of all, we can teach parents and teachers how they can facilitate that change to help their children succeed at school and in life. Immature reflexes, underdeveloped senses and poor motor development, and incomplete brain connections can be developed and improved to maturity.

Brain Gym® and the Rhythmic Movement Training programs involve personal one-on-one sessions and workshops for parents, teachers and other health professionals. These programs assist a child to be better prepared for academic learning. Learning gaps in children's physical development can be dramatically improved which in turn helps them to develop, mature and heal physically, emotionally and mentally. Behaviour improves dramatically.

Here is a testimonial from a parent:

> *"Our daughter was very volatile, easily distracted and moody. Her behaviour was so erratic that we spent months working with a child psychologist. While she was well behaved at school, her grades were low, she was easily distracted and had poor concentration.*
>
> *We first heard about Enza's work through a friend. After Tayla's first session, we noticed an immediate change in her behaviour.*
>
> *Following two sessions of Brain Gym® and Rhythmic Movement Training with Enza, Tayla's a totally different girl. She is calmer, more centred and loving. Her concentration is stronger and her report card has risen from Bs and Cs to As and Bs. Consequently, she is more confident, less critical of herself and such a delightful little girl.*
>
> *What an amazing transformation! I highly recommend Enza's services."* Janice, HR Manager, Mother

Some of you might be wondering by now what exactly causes ADHD. The answer, unfortunately, is not as cut and dried as you might want it to be. I will cover this topic in the next chapter.

CHAPTER 4

What could be the possible causes of ADD / ADHD?

It is only natural that parents who are told that their child has been diagnosed as having Attention Deficit Hyperactivity Disorder (ADHD) will want to know exactly what went wrong.

A definitive cause of ADHD has yet to be identified. It is likely that inherited genetic factors play a role. Other factors that have been associated with ADHD include premature birth, maternal alcohol and tobacco use, exposure to high levels of lead in early childhood and brain injuries, especially those that involve the prefrontal cortex. There is also over stimulation from excessive exposure to EMF's from computers, TV, video games, electronic games and not playing outside anymore.

Recent breakthroughs in the study of the brain, using neural imaging, has revealed links between ADHD and:

> brain structure

> the function of chemicals in the brain that help regulate attention and activity

> differences in function of some of the areas of the brain that affect attention and impulse control

Studies conducted by the National Institute of Mental Health in

U.S.A. found that the right prefrontal cortex, two basal ganglia and the vermis region of the cerebellum are significantly smaller than normal in children with ADHD. These findings make sense because the brain areas that are reduced in size in children with ADHD are the very ones that regulate attention, help restrain behaviour and control mood.

Studies have also shown that children with ADHD have less activity and blood flow in these important frontal lobe areas of the brain. In addition, there is evidence linking the malfunction of neurotransmitters, which help transmit signals between nerves, and ADHD.

Although the source of these problems is yet to be conclusively proven, it is worthwhile to consider the factors which may contribute to developmental problems in the brain. The brain is primarily a sensory processing machine that is constantly collecting and organising information received from the external world. Neuroscience has shown that brain development relies on interaction with the surrounding environment through the senses and movement. The richer that experience, the more new nerve cells and neural connections are formed throughout the whole brain.

However, there is a 'short circuit' in the brain which, in certain circumstances, causes nerve activity to be centred in the survival centres of the mind and body, and thereby limits activation of the frontal lobes. This 'short circuit' is the primal survival response – the flight or fight mechanism.

In her book *Smart Moves*, Carla Hannaford PhD (neurobiologist) notes that, "in times of real danger, these survival instincts are invaluable... but the response does not make us smart, creative or rational." Modern living rarely requires the activation of the survival response. Yet, stress from various environmental and social influences can trigger the survival response and consequently limit frontal lobe brain development.

The frontal lobe of the brain controls fine motor movement, inner speech, self control and reasoning. Exposure to stress affects this part of the brain. Consequently, stressed out, survival oriented humans have less opportunity to develop nerve net into the frontal lobe and may exhibit learning difficulties as a result.

Carla Hannaford, PhD, details these stressors, including:

Developmental – premature birth, brain injury inflicted during delivery, hereditary factors, disease, lack of sensory stimulation and movement, lack of touch, being left alone without tactile or vestibular stimulation, forced to spend time in baby walkers and car seats instead of moving around on the floor, lack of interactive creative play and communication

Nutritional – inadequate suitable nutrition for brain development, inadequate water or oxygen, chemicals and heavy metal toxicity from pesticides on foods and environment

Electrical – excessive exposure to external EMF's TV, Computers and video – over stimulation which can lead to violence, decreased imaginative development, ocular lock, decreased motor development

Competition – inappropriate pressure to perform at school and at home, competition in sports and in the arts, learning in a winner/loser mindset rather than cooperative win/win

Educational systems – developmentally inappropriate curricula, constant low-level skills testing, unawareness of unique learning styles.

The precise causes of ADHD may not be known, but it seems clear that addressing factors that inhibit brain development and learning can only be beneficial.

The developmental stages of an infant

Let's look at a few examples on how to recognize a reflex, if the reflex is still retained and not integrated by a certain time and how it will affect a child or adult in their movement and learning.

In order to survive an infant is equipped with primitive reflexes designed to ensure immediate response to its new environment. Primitive reflexes are automatic, stereotyped movements directed by the brain stem. They are essential for the child's survival for the first few weeks of the infant's life. The primitive reflexes emerge in utero, are present at birth and should be inhibited by six months of age to twelve months at the latest. Prolonged primitive reflex activity may prevent the development of the succeeding postural reflexes. If the primitive reflexes are retained, it is evident of structural weakness or immaturity of the central nervous system.

Through my research and study I have learnt that the stages of child development lay the foundation for accurate intentional movements and setting up of the internal wiring of the brain. Once the movement is integrated we are able to perform the movement easily. If this does not occur the child will find it difficult to read, write, focus, concentrate and sit still. It's like one parent described it as "having an infant still active within a 9 year old child".

The vestibular system is a special sensory apparatus in our inner ear. This body balance mechanism helps us to know where up is so we can maintain equilibrium. Effective vestibular training from whole body movements like hopping, skipping, rolling dancing, tumbling, running and slow cross crawling movements will assist in its development. A child with vestibular difficulties can't sit still. They move in order to know where they are in space. The vestibular is activated whenever the body and head moves and helps to relate to gravity.

The vestibular is connected to the Reticular Activating System. If there is a weakness in the system, information will not go to the senses and then to the cortex, the thinking part of the brain. A child who hops, skips and jumps is stimulating their vestibular system. A child who can't sit still instinctively know they need to get moving to acquire balance. The most advanced level of the vestibular development is stillness. Some children who are not able to stand on one leg means the vestibular system is not functioning adequately. Many adults have that challenge which can be improved with Brain Gym® and Rhythmic Movement Training.

Vision, hearing, gross fine motor coordination, eye hand coordination, body awareness, being able to cross the midline is what develops through reflexes, sensory and motor development.

How to recognize a retained reflex
Each infant reflex movement is triggered by a sound, touch and change of position. When the reflex is triggered it causes an involuntary movement. It is said to be retained. Children, teens and adults who can't sit still have retain reflexes still present in the body.

Root and Suck Reflex
When an infant's cheek is touched the mouth moves towards the hand or nipple. It is present at birth and integrated by four months. If this reflex is retained the child may have a hard time articulating words, chews and bites objects. He is oversensitive to touch on his cheek or mouth and have difficulty taking in nourishment seemingly being a fussy eater.

Moro Reflex

When an infant hears a sudden sound he will throw his arms out and take in a quick gasp of air and slowly draw his arms back in towards his body. This reflex should integrate at two to four months. When retained the child may overreact to fears and startles at nearly every sudden sound.

Fear Paralysis

The infant has a tendency to retreat from anything threatening. This is to be integrated by the time of birth. With my experience I have found it can still be retained in adults in a stressful environment causing fear paralysis. A child would be extremely shy and avoid eye contact. They are hypersensitive and uncomfortable in tight clothing.

Palmar Reflex

A touch on the inside of the infants hand causes him to grip very hard and may cause mouth or tongue to move when manipulating objects for example an open mouth response when catching a ball. This reflex should be integrated by two to three months. If not, it will show in a child having poor manual dexterity, holds a pencil in a tense fist like grip, moves tongue and mouth while writing.

Spinal Galant Reflex

A touch on the infant's side near the waist triggers a pulling away movement. This reflex should integrate by three to nine months. A child with this retained reflex can't sit still, easily tickled, doesn't rest against his chair, dislikes elastic waistbands and tight clothing and wet or soil himself.

Tonic Labyrinthine Reflex (TLR)

Forward movement of head causes the infant's arms and legs to bend: backward movement causes the arms and legs to extend.

This reflex should integrate by four months. If this reflex is retained some children will have low muscle tone, the child will slouch and prop up the head on his hand while writing. He will struggle with sequencing, organisation skills, short term memory, difficulty focusing near and far.

Asymmetrical Tonic Neck Reflex (ATNR)
When the infant turns his head, his arm and legs extend and follow while opposite side draws into the body. This reflex should be integrated by six months. If this reflex is retained a child will struggle to concentrate, tying shoes, balancing and ball catching.

Symmetrical Tonic Neck Reflex(STNR)
Backward movement of the head causes the arms to straighten hip and legs to bend. This reflex should be integrated by nine to eleven months. A child with retained STNR would have difficulty focusing in the classroom, wriggling in his chair and does not want to stay on his chair.

In order to resolve these issues with retained reflexes, Brain Gym® and Rhythmic Movement Training can effectively integrate the reflexes. It does not need to be a lengthy session. Some reflexes are mildly retained and children can respond quickly using the simple five step repatterning balance process. Children enjoy doing the movements. These programs are very successful in integrating the reflexes allowing the child to improve learning, coordination and behaviour.

Here is Hayden's story:

"My son, Hayden, aged six year old, has been diagnosed with ADHD and Aspergers. Hayden has been visiting a speech therapist, occupational therapist and psychiatrists on a regular basis. I attended end of term meeting with Hayden's school teacher to find out that Hayden was falling behind his class and was not interested in learning. Hayden's school has suggested that I should look at other school options as they did not know how to teach him. I knew I had to find another solution. After moving house I found a box of items full of my special memories and books from when I was a child. I came across a book called "Switch on your Brain" by Dr Paul Dennison. It came to me that Hayden needed help with Brain Gym° just like when I did when I was eight years old which I had positive results through my schooling years. After three appointments with Enza I have noticed the following changes: starting to recognize sight words, wanting to learn, controlled behaviour and higher concentration levels. We spent a 15 minutes a day doing Brain Gym° and Rhythmic movements diligently. Last month, Hayden had received two first places in the school sports carnival, a determination award from his school teacher. When he attends little Athletics he no longer has emotional outbursts and is very interactive with his friends." — Marilyn, Mother

CHAPTER 5

Smart nutrition

As previously discussed, recent breakthroughs in the study of the brain using neural imaging have demonstrated the connection between brain development and ADHD.

Although the source of these problems is yet to be conclusively proven, the evidence is mounting that the wrong diet can cripple brain function while switching to the right 'brain power' foods can produce amazing results.

Of course, even without all the science, common sense says that anything that can improve the health of the brain, and assist with its optimal development, will be beneficial.

As you would expect, brain cells are the most sophisticated and nutritionally demanding cells in the body. When the right foods are provided to nourish a child's brain and body, they are better able to activate their innate potential for healing and learning.

Avoid brain stressors

When considering the sources of stress on the brain, it is important to remember the brain-body connection. The brain is a complex organ that draws on the energy provided by what we eat, and interacts with every other system in the body.

The brain is incredibly sensitive to toxicity introduced into the body through high fat, high sugar, high carbohydrate, low nutrition fast food and unhealthy snacks (often called 'hyper-food'). Another source is chemically laden processed foods with additives, colours, preservatives, heavy metals and pesticide contamination. Personal care products, cosmetics, household cleaning products and pesticide chemicals also have the potential to cause serious health problems.

Hair Tissue Mineral Analysis research reveals a strong relationship between hyperactivity in children and toxic metal such as cadmium, lead and mercury as well as high levels of iron, manganese and copper. Deficiencies of certain minerals have been shown to be associated with decreased academic performance. If you would like more information on Hair Tissue Mineral Analysis I encourage you to contact me at www.dlhc.com.au. It could make the difference.

In addition, the health of the brain is closely connected to the health of the gastrointestinal tract. When the gut is not working properly to pass waste out of the body, this can introduce additional toxicity into the body and place stress on the immune system and liver. Therefore a diet designed for optimal brain performance must also take into account what is needed for a healthy gut.

Nourish and fuel your brain for success

For optimal brain performance, and overall health, the best diet is one that incorporates a balanced variety of fresh, natural foods including whole grains, fruit and vegetables, quality calcium sources, quality protein sources and healthy oils.

Phytochemicals are essential for optimal brain function and diminishes the risk of disease. They are abundant in fresh vegetables. Many nutritionists are talking about important it is to have green drinks made of fresh organically grown green vegetables. Our fondness of processed and overcooked foods show that many peoples' diets are lacking in life-giving phytochemicals. Adding green food extract powder into a drink or in capsule form is a quick easy way to get phytochemcials in your body.

One of the best food supplements with all the minerals our body needs is *Algotene*, a red marine Phytoplankton, also called whole dried *Dunaliella salina*, which is grown in Australia. This product helps maintain vitality, healthy immune system, skin and eyes. On a gram per gram basis, Dunaliella salina can contain more than twice the chlorophyll of Spirulina, 8 times the mineral content and over 6,000 times the antioxidant content. *Dunaliella salina* contains a rich mixture of natural dietary carotenoids including extremely high quantities of antioxidant beta-carotene, a deep orange-red pigment also found in carrots and apricots. *Dunaliella salina*, also contains a spectrum of other health and vitality boosting phytonutirents including proteins, amino acids, essential fatty acids, carbohydrates, vitamins, minerals and cholorophyll. Check www.dlhc.com.au for more information.

It is especially important to supplement with the following brain power foods: omega three fatty acids, omega six fatty acids, iron, calcium, magnesium, zinc and B vitamins. For example food supplements such as good quality fish oil.

You may ask the question, how do I know how much and what type of supplement I need to give my child? A Hair Tissue Mineral Analysis test can help pinpoint metabolic disturbances as well as indicate the appropriate nutritional approach. A hair analysis report gives you reliable clinical data on over thirty-five nutrient and toxic minerals and over twenty-six significant mineral ratios. It is safe, scientific, non-invasive, identifies potential nutrient mineral deficiencies and excesses, indicates toxic mineral exposure, highlights concern and recommends suitable dietary changes and supplements for improved health. To find out more about Hair Tissue Mineral Analysis testing please contact me and I can assist you or check out where you can do it in your area.

Probiotics help the gut stay healthy to reduce stress and aid in detoxification. Many health practitioners agree that leaky gut can cause a wide range of problems including fatigue, mood-wings, irritability, hyperactivity, poor coordination, muscle or joint pain, memory difficulties, food sensitivities, sleep disturbances and environmental intolerances. The definition of a Leaky Gut Syndrome is a gastrointestinal tract dysfunction caused by antibiotics, lack of probiotics, toxins, poor diet, injestion of junk foods (fried foods and sugar laden foods), severe emotional stress or trauma, gastrointestinal parasites or infections, leading to increased intestinal wall permeability and absorption of toxins, bacteria, fungi, parasites, intestinal bacterial infections and overgrowth and nutritional deficiencies.

Including Probiotics bacteria (friendly flora) can help neutralize toxins in the gut and create healing with a leaky gut. Ultimately, it will improve the immune system. Yoghurt is a great food but unfortunately the friendly bacteria it provides does not survive in the gastrointestinal tract. You need to continually replenish the friendly bacteria. Check at the store for good quality probiotics capsules or powders that deliver longer lasting benefits and that you can regularly incorporate into your diet.

Eliminate and cleanse

Finally, plenty of clean filtered water (not juices or fizzy drinks) is critical for the brain and gut. Water assists in taking nutrition into the cells and eliminating toxins out of the body.

Take note if your child has reactions to certain foods, then eliminate them for a short period of time. Identify and managing food allergies or intolerances can bring about dramatic improvements in performance and overall health.

Using the nutritional approach

Foods to avoid if allergic reactions

Many children today have allergic reactions to wheat, corn, soy, dairy, eggs, yeast, sugar, preservatives, food additives (artificial sweeteners like aspartame and saccharin, sodium lauryl suphate, MSG, yellow dyes, nitrates and others), chocolate, peanuts and certain fruits like oranges. Be attentive as these foods, chemicals, additives and preservatives can cause serious reactions. Test, eliminate and detoxify. There are so many choices of foods today to replace the ones we take out.

Is your child suffering from dry skin, acne, candidiasis or eczema? I use Hair Analysis to find whether the skin is related to chemical toxins that are causing a reaction because of an underlying nutrient deficiency. If it is toxins, with Nutritional Energy Balancing of blocked meridians, the technique can balance the body's over reactivity to toxins, identifying the correct toxin and eliminating contact can massively aid the skin to repair. If the skin is nutritionally deficient it may be the body blocking natural absorption of nutrients essential to healthy skin. Releasing meridian blockage can allow the body full absorption of its required nutrition.

Furthermore adrenal and emotional stress may inhibit the body's energy to absorb full nutrition, a client may require other techniques to help the reactivity to emotional stress and reduce the physiological reaction to emotions. Emotional stress can lead to the body system's dysfunction or can be leading to reflect in poor skin quality. There are also natural products that can remove chemicals and heavy metals out of the cells so it can improve digestion, health and clarity of mind.

Food choices

There are many choices of food to eat. The alternative choices of wheat and corn are grains such as rice, millet, buckwheat, amaranth, quinoa, rolled oats, rye, chia and others. There is such a variety of fruits and vegetables, sweet potatoes, meat, poultry, (except processed meats with nitrates), fish, beans, nuts, seeds (sunflower), sweeteners like honey, stevia, pure maple syrup, brown rice syrup and many more depending what country you live in. Eating foods with high fibre (vegetable, fruit and grains) acts as a broom sweeping toxins out of the body. Eat fresh organically grown foods whenever possible.

To eliminate gut parasites and other unfriendly microbes can improve health and the immune system. Some people take small amounts of colloidal silver to eliminating parasites, fungi and unfriendly bacteria out of the body. There are also Chinese herb supplements that work well.

With the correct diet, children will be calmer, more positive, better able to focus, and more responsive to further learning and behavioural therapies. It is always advisable to check with nutritionist or a health care professional.

Now, there are many emotions that can come about when you have a child who has been diagnosed with ADHD. How do you deal with these?

CHAPTER 6

The hidden danger sabotaging your child's learning

There are many factors that may contribute to your child experiencing ADD, ADHD and early learning difficulties. Stress is one which is often overlooked.

We like to think of childhood as a time of carefree play, unburdened by adult responsibilities. However, in our modern, fast-paced society, our every activity from a very young age is scheduled, scrutinised and measured. Whether it's getting better grades, winning the grand final, or having lots of friends, there are many situations in which children feel pressure to perform.

Moreover, why, when we are so frequently stressed by our relationships, finances and careers (just to name a few common concerns), would we think that children are immune to this influence?

In fact, stress and anxiety is a real problem for children and can certainly contribute to serious early learning difficulties, or delayed development of important educational skills such as learning to read and write. It can also impact on children's long-term health and well-being.

> ➢ Does your child display the danger signs of stress and anxiety?

> ➢ Does your child complain about headaches and pains in the neck, shoulders or jaw?

➢ Does your child have bad dreams or wet the bed?

➢ Does your child have difficulty adapting to change and do they question what will happen in the future?

➢ Does your child have difficulty understanding instructions and often appear distracted?

How does stress and anxiety sabotage your child's learning?

"Stress is a reaction of perceived threat. The stress response prepares the individual to mentally and physically take protective action... But the stress response does not make us smart, creative or rational." Carla Hannaford PhD (Neurobiologist)

Your child's ability to learn is directly impacted when they are under stress, because the stress response: decreases blood flow to the higher areas of the brain that have to do with planning, memory, insight and learning, increases muscle tension throughout the body which can lead to chronic pain and digestive problems, increases heart rate to distribute oxygen around the body, thereby reducing oxygen available to the brain, dilates pupils to increase peripheral vision and heighten awareness of potential danger, thereby reducing reading abilities, induces hypersensitivity to sound to heighten awareness of potential danger, thereby reducing ability to concentrate on instructions and take reasoned action.

Deactivating the stress response for successful learning

It is clear that stress and anxiety can be key contributors to children's early learning difficulties, or to other developmental problems they may experience with socialization, literacy and physical coordination.

For this reason, Brain Gym® and Rhythmic Movement Training incorporates techniques that empower children to:

➢ work through whatever anxieties or fears are holding them back

➢ gain confidence with fun, easy exercises

➢ engage higher reasoning to overcome any problem or stressful situation

➢ activate the mind-body connection for calm, relaxed focus.

For your child's success, parents be aware of your child's stress levels and consider ways you can empower them to become calmer and happier every day.

Finding the way out of stress

Now we know stress actually inhibits our ability to deal with challenges, both big and small, and can cause long-term damage to our health and well-being.

Often we try to escape stress by distracting ourselves from the unpleasant emotions or situations causing stress, and by switching off our minds and bodies altogether. TV, the internet, alcohol and caffeine can provide this kind of escape. However, this does not switch off the stress response – sometimes it makes us numb to what is happening, but in most cases it makes the problem worse.

The best strategy to switch off the stress response is to work with the mind and body to bring it back to its natural state – calm, fully present, focused and connected to others and the surrounding environment. By doing the Brain Gym® exercises which relaxes the body leading to a more helpful brain chemistry for confident and clear thinking.

The following suggestions all work to calm the mind and body, whilst also activating and enhancing our mind-body connection.

Top five tips to switch off your stress response as a parent

1. Take a 15 minute walk outside, preferably somewhere green, and give attention to all your senses. What can you hear, see, smell and feel?

2. Get moving! Dance, stretch or practice simple Brain Gym® movements such as touching your right elbow to your left knee and then left elbow to your right knee in a slow, conscious manner. Also, doing Brain Buttons and Hook-ups helps to relax the body.

3. Adjust the volume. Put on a favourite song and sing along, or try some soothing nature sounds, or turn off all the noise (ipods, phones and TV's) and sit quietly focusing on the sound of your breath.

4. Dim the lights or perhaps bring out a scented oil burner. Gently cover your eyes with your hands and rest.

5. Focus on what is right in your life. Write a gratitude list of things you are thankful for.

You can empower your children by teaching these simple tips so they can learn to deactivate their stress whenever they want to. Make time to do the activities with your child. They will love you for it.

Bonus tip: Choose whatever feels right for you, with full consciousness of what your body and your mind needs. Check-in with yourself and be gentle and forgiving.

CHAPTER 7

Making time for genuine play

We are all living increasingly fast paced lives. Ask any parent if they feel harassed, frustrated, short of time or tired on a daily basis and they will most certainly answer, 'YES!'

The success of any activity in our modern world seems to be measured in terms of efficiency or economy: 'how much work did I finish today or how much money did I make?' There's pressure to do more, to work more productively, to fill available time with something 'worthwhile'. So-called relaxation time becomes another chore to be slotted into an already over-flowing schedule. Often, rather than true relaxation, we rely on distracting ourselves from our busy lives with the TV or internet – neither of which totally contributes to a peaceful state of mind.

Children learn from the parents behaviour, and the world around them. Soon their natural desire for genuine, child-like play is distorted to a search for constant stimulation through high intensity activities such as TV, video games and over-excited, competitive interaction with other kids.

Most parents and educators instinctively know that kids do better, in school and in life, if they spend less time 'vegging out' in front of the TV and more time playing, more time outside and more time interacting with others. But why is that the case?

Neuroscience has shown that the development of the brain, from when we are babies, relies on interaction with the surrounding environment through our senses and through movement. Each interaction, each new movement and experience, activates new neural connections in our brain. The targeted movements of Brain Gym have been created to aid in this activation. As we stimulate and grow our brain in this way, we train our brain to think and learn better.

What do we mean by genuine play?

Isn't all play the same? As long as kids are outside – playing competitive sport for example – doesn't that equate with play?

> *Take a moment and think back to your childhood... Do you remember a day spent playing with family or friends? Perhaps you were camping, or at the beach, or just in a neighbourhood garden. The day unfolded magically as you melded role playing and creating from the environment around you and energetic movement. Of course, you didn't think of it that way. You were simply spacemen, or fairies at the bottom of the garden, or underwater explorers. There were no rules, or only the ones made up as you went along. Did you chase, and take turns, and tumble in the grass and lie on your backs spotting shapes in the clouds drifting by? Everything seemed full of colour and smell and sound, and when you were called back inside it was like the whole day flew by in a few minutes.*

How do you feel now, remembering that day? Relaxed? Happy?

Carla Hannaford PhD (neurobiologist and educator) says that play is 'spontaneous, connected, explorative, safe, non-competitive, lost-in-the-moment, balanced, rough and tumble, joyful play that creates a moment of bliss and flow.'

Stuart L Brown (MD and psychiatrist) adds that it is an 'intrinsically pleasurable activity, free of anxiety or other over powering emotion, without a visible, clear-cut goal other than its own activity.'

Play is not highly structured or over planned, and it's not the same as time spent on competitive sports, computer games or educational toys.

Why is genuine play so important to your child's health, happiness and learning?

The brain is primarily a sensory processing machine that is constantly collecting and organising the information we receive from the world around us. Neuroscience has shown that the development of the brain, from when we are babies, relies on interaction with the surrounding environment through our senses and through movement. The richer our experience, the more new nerve cells and neural connections are formed, and these are the superhighways for intellectual and physical performance.

Play engages all our senses and sparks a whole range of new movements – delivering a gold mine of information for learning and brain development. This has also been shown in the laboratory where the rats and mice with the most enriched environments, with room for movement and companions for play, display the most nerve cell growth – even in older rats and mice.

> *The true story of Brandy is a powerful illustration of the power of play. Brandy was a vibrant, intelligent, happy child who suddenly started having seizures at the age of four. The seizures became so frequent (over 100/day) that she became totally incapacitated. After the failure of all available treatments it was decided to take the radical action of removing the whole right hemisphere of Brandy's brain, leaving the entire left side of her body paralysed.*

> *Though this cured the seizures, it left Brandy and her family devastated. How could she live a full life with only half a brain? On the advice of one doctor, the family began to challenge Brandy's body and senses through physical therapy, lots of massage, music, reading to her, nature walks and lots of play – totally enriching her environment. By the age of 14, Brandy was a bright, straight A student, who rode horses and even danced. Her story forced scientists of the day to reconsider the power of the brain and the role of movement and play in development.*
>
> From *'Awakening the Child Heart'* by Carla Hannaford PhD.

Five top tips for great play with your child

1. Babies are be allowed to move freely on the floor as much as possible and encouraged to roll around and explore their environment. As they grow, do not limit their experience to only bright toys, let them play (as they are naturally driven to do) with all sorts of day-to-day objects and provide varied sensations such as mud, shells and sand. Interaction with others through touch is also important.

2. Swinging and spinning are key movements in the development of the brain and co-ordination. Unfortunately, concerns about safety has meant the forbidding of the 'risky' activities that encourage just this kind of movement. Think swings, merry go rounds, climbing trees, rolling down hills, walking on fences and trampolines. A newly popularised tool that uses circular movement to activate balance in the brain is the ancient labyrinth – a spiral path marked out on the ground with equal numbers of left and right turns. You may find one in a park or local school, or you can easily build your own with instructions from the internet.

3. Seek out opportunities for active play that encourages flow and connection with others such as nature walks, bike riding, ball games, tennis, volleyball and swimming. Brain Gym movements can be done together, they are fun, simple exercises that activate the brain for better learning and development.

4. Whatever you are doing, be alert for opportunities to engage the senses in the surrounding environment:

   - What can you see? Play a game of I spy or take turns creating stories incorporating everyday elements you can see.
   - What can you hear? Listen for nature and urban sounds. Wonder what is making the sound and what it might look like. Use voice to imitate the sound or make up a song about it.
   - Keep going... What can you taste? What can you smell? What can you feel?

5. Most importantly, have fun! Laughter increases blood flow to the brain, increases heart rate and increases tolerance to pain and discomfort. Create space for carefree play without deadlines and schedules. With your child, acknowledge when you have had a good time with appreciation and gratitude. Recall how much fun you had later in the day, perhaps at bedtime.

Play is so important in the development of our children – so remember to slow down and enjoy play for your child's health, happiness and learning!

CHAPTER 8

Three basic principles for making behaviour changes

Do you make New Year's Resolutions? Alternatively, have you made a goal to lose XX number of pounds or kilos, before your birthday? Did you make it—or did you struggle with changing the behaviour that caused the problem to begin with? Either way, you certainly can understand how difficult changing ingrained behaviours can be. Making lasting changes typically involves a commitment by all the parties involved, and takes time and lots of effort.

Some parents with ADHD-affected children have tried many techniques through trial and error processes, and failed to get any lasting results. This can be disheartening and sometimes causes them to just give up and believe they will have to live with the inappropriate behaviour.

Many medical practitioners today are championing behavioural therapy for the treatment of ADHD; they believe that by encouraging behaviour modifications they can help parents to minimise the symptoms, and the frustrations, of living with someone with ADHD. There are three main components for behavioural treatment such as this—finding and developing talent, structure, and lifestyle changes - rather than focusing on medication.

Finding and developing talent

One of the most important steps in this process is to find something that the child is good at, and to develop that talent. Rather than finding fault with him or her and pointing out obvious flaws, and how he or she is different, instead nurture those abilities that give the child pleasure.

Does your child love to draw? Encourage them to draw and paint by buying them art supplies, taking them to art museums, and signing them up for classes. Is he or she a more physical type that likes to ride bikes? Why not allow them to plan some trail excursions? They will enjoy it, and be happy that you allowed them to make the plans and that you came with them. Is hiking their forte? Buy some hiking boots for you both, and find the nearest parks! It will do you both some good.

The point is that your child has some interests, things that will keep his or her attention. Find out what those things are and encourage them to develop in those areas. Channel all that excess energy into something productive and you will both feel less frustrated.

Structure

Lack of structure in the life of a child who suffers from ADHD is a huge mistake as well; planning out each step necessary to accomplish a task can help tremendously toward their success. Make a list of what needs to be done; it gives him or her a place to check for expectations, and for what to do next. With most children, taking each day as it comes is okay, but with these children that can lead to lots of frustration and battles. It is better that they know in advance, what will happen and what your expectations are for them. Keep everything brief and to the point with them, as their attention will drift if instructions ramble. In other words, break tasks down into small chunks for best results.

Work together with everyone that is involved in your child's development; this means the school, his or her doctor, other family members, and any other people that are a part of their life on a regular basis. Speak with everyone involved and make sure that everyone is working toward the same objectives. Keeping a journal that goes to school and back daily can help you to communicate with teachers, and vice versa. Just letting each other know what the child's behaviour was like that day can give you clues as to what to expect.

This provides a written record to share with healthcare practitioners also, and can shed some light on what happens at certain times that might cause different behaviours. You might be able to pinpoint certain situations, places, or even people that seem to aggravate his or her behaviour. If so, removing them from the inciting "thing" can become a simple matter.

Like other children, a very effective tool is to emphasize the positive and ignore or downplay those negative things. Because these children are so used to hearing "no", they often respond almost miraculously to someone gloating about them. It is a challenge, but focusing on what the child is doing right will take you a long way towards encouraging more of that behaviour.

One effective technique is "labeled praise." This means praise that also clearly tells them what you like about what they did. "You did an awesome job raking up those leaves" is a lot more helpful to them than a simple "Thanks for helping" would be.

Lifestyle changes

Another successful technique is token economics. Schools are using this increasingly to promote and reward good behaviour. Critics feel it is ridiculous to reward a child for exhibiting the behaviour that is expected, and think it is condescending. However, for kids with ADHD, reinforcement gives them something tangible to anticipate.

Keep an open mind when considering techniques and lifestyle changes to help children with ADHD. These children have critical difficulties controlling their behaviour; their brain might tell them to do the right thing, while their disorder stops those signals from getting through to them.

A system that allows children to earn points in school and at home can work very well for children with ADHD. Allow them to help you put it together, and let them decide on the types of rewards that would appeal to them—this can be extra privileges or other types of rewards. For instance, if they like to ice skate, perhaps a certain number of points would earn them an afternoon of skating, or a computer buff could earn an hour of computer time. These rewards can be great incentives to alter their behaviour for the better, especially when the rewards are things they love.

Children in general have naturally short attention spans, so giving immediate praise for good behaviour can make a huge difference. In the case of behaviour you would like to change, you have to be very clear and specific about what you need to change, and talk to them as soon after the behaviour as practical. Kids with ADHD crave feedback. When giving praise or a compliment, spell out exactly why you are happy with the behaviour and what he or she has done to earn it. Physical affection—hugs, an extra privilege, or a special treat they enjoy substituted at intervals can work well also.

Children with ADHD need good rewards to motivate them because they are desensitized to most things. Rewards that are more important will encourage them to follow the rules, perform as expected, or behave properly, so make them worth earning.

When a child has had a mixture of good and bad behaviour, always give them praise for their good behaviours before talking about any negative issues. Never make punishment the first step—and when necessary, try to make it mild and always specific to the negative behaviour.

The most important thing for parents is to maintain consistency. Some parents tend to give in far too often, and at the wrong times. Try to react the same to a certain behaviour when it happens, so that they learn to anticipate whether you will be pleased or displeased at certain intervals.

Children with ADHD are often disobedient, so being persistent can be difficult. In fact, it might often seem that all your efforts are for naught, and you will end up frustrated and miserable, if you do not take control of the situation.

Stick to your guns when it comes to praise and discipline. You and other authority figures must respond the same to a behaviour whether at home, at school, church, or the local playground. In fact, allowing a child to "divide and conquer" gives him or her the upper hand—exactly the situation you do not want.

No matter where you are, or who is present, respond in exactly the same way to a behaviour issue. The rules, the rewards, and any negative consequences need to always be the same. These children need that consistency in their lives.

Never contradict or undermine another parent or other authority figure in the presence of the child. Cohesiveness is vital; without it, the child will be confused, and you will all stop moving forward. In other words, you are not helping your child at all if you allow this to happen.

Always be ready to handle problems that arise. Despite your best efforts, children with ADHD can be disruptive and troublesome in public places, which can be embarrassing for the parents. Always anticipate things that might happen so that you are prepared to deal with them, and so that you can prepare clear rules for your child's behaviour and communicate them succinctly. If parent and child both know what to expect, things will go much smoother.

Keeping things in perspective is important; dealing with an ADHD child is difficult. Parents of these children can be frustrated, angry, and embarrassed, and they can feel hopeless. Remembering at all times that you are the adult and must maintain control is vital to keeping the situation from spiraling rapidly out of control. ADHD children have a medical issue and are unable to control their behaviour at times.

Become a serious list-maker; teach your child to make lists as well. Write down any tasks that need to be done, events to attend, or any other details that are important. Especially for your child, making a list of what they need to do, including any steps that need to be taken to complete them, help them build their critical thinking skills. Later, when completing the tasks, encourage them to check each thing off their list, which gives them a sense of accomplishment.

When you realize that kids with ADHD tend to brush off anything besides what is right in front of them at the time, completing a list of tasks is a momentous event. You might give them a surprise reward when they complete a list of tasks—a celebratory hug and run to the local ice cream store does not cost much in terms of time or money, but goes a long way toward reinforcing the lifestyle changes you want. When they realize what they are capable of, and see how happy it makes you, they will repeat the performance until it eventually becomes a habit.

It is true that children with ADHD have boundless energy, and for that reason, you need to provide outlets for this excess. Give them many opportunities for physical exercise, and encourage them in hobbies or other activities that let them blow off steam.

Accept your child's limitations; this is an important coping strategy. A child with ADHD will likely never be the model child among his peers—accept it, and make things the best you can for you and your child. See your child's positive attributes and embrace them, encouraging him or her to make the most of every gift given to them.

You are the expert when it comes to your child, and his or her specific behavioural issues. Not all ADHD children are the same, and they do not all respond the same to stimuli or situations. It is a controversial subject, and everyone has an opinion; ignore those that obviously have no clue about the situation or are negative. Trust your individual instincts and always keep the lines of communication open with your child. Continually monitor the situation and be observant because your guidance is what will make your child's, and your, life better. ADHD is different for each child, and it is vital to know which problems are truly parts of ADHD, so that all issues can be properly handled.

Avoid labels. Look at your child as just that—your child. He or she has his own personality, his own talents, his own interests, and yes, his own behavioural issues. Just do not allow the label to overshadow everything positive about your child.

Another problem that ADHD parents sometimes have is to lump all of a child's problems—whether it is anxiety, learning problems, or depression—as being part of his ADHD. If there are other issues, they need to be addressed separately. Experts are improving their abilities to separate ADHD and learning disabilities, even though they can sometimes overlap.

Stay calm when dealing with an ADHD child above all over things. Speak slowly and clearly, and let them know that you will always be calm and in charge, even in the face of massive frustration. Children learn a lot by observation. Talking with them and allowing them to see how you envision things going can give them some of the tools they need to control themselves just as well.

When it gets to be a little too much for you, take a break! Living with, working with, and loving a child with ADHD is exhausting! Be sure that you have some time for yourself by finding a reliable sitter or signing them up for a class or workshop, or a Scout troop. Be sure that you have some respite care.

Brain Gym movements done together will help with bonding between the two of you, and also relax and calm you both. Make use of them and you will find some relief.

CHAPTER 9

Practical parenting strategies

When you are the parent of a child with ADHD, there are many more difficulties than there are with the average child. Experimenting to see what works best for your child, and your family, is important. Keep in mind, though, that what works one day may not on another due to their unpredictability.

The way you deal with your child affects the way your child behaves. Good habits can be reinforced and learnt, and just as easily, you can do things that will reinforce bad behaviour:

Perpetuating the treatment you received as a child; do not yell or hit your child because it was done to you. Do not go to the opposite extreme disciplining your child, however. He or she needs firm rules and structure.

Parents fighting against each other. If you and your spouse or other family members disagree on rules, keep it out of the child's earshot. It will confuse the child and also set up a divide and conquer system, inevitably causing rapid deterioration in behaviour.

Low energy supplies. Working hard at your job, not getting enough sleep, or coming down with the flu can cause you to let discipline lapse. While infrequent instances will not hurt, extended periods will cause bad behaviour, because your child is not getting direction from you, or your attention.

Fighting and nagging. Because of your child's behavioural problems, you might spend a lot of time arguing and nagging your child. Do not allow that to ruin your entire relationship! Be sure that you have fun together, too.

Make "dates" with your child to spend time doing things you both enjoy, or simply play together. You can use these times to teach your child about rules, what is acceptable, and what is not. For example, teaching your child to keep his hands to himself is important, so that he does not hit, bite, or punch other children. If he does not learn these things, he will have a hard time making friends and the other kids will ignore him.

Just a generation ago, children were told they should be "seen and not heard," and when they broke a rule, they often got a sharp swat with a wooden spoon or the switch from a tree. We realize today that children, like all people, respond much better to love and affection, feeling secure and important to their parents. We also know that reinforcing positive behaviour works better than punishing their bad behaviours. Some children misbehave simply because it is the only time they get attention, and what happens bad attention is better than none at all. Remember with loving intention, firm rules and structure

Negotiate rules with older children and allow them to have a say in what happens.

Be consistent with rules. Clearly state what you expect—finish your homework before you go out to play. If they challenge it or disregard the rule, remind them of the consequences. Perhaps they are not allowed to play their game for a day when they do not follow the rules. Enforce the rule if necessary; even if that means unplugging the game unit and putting it away.

Pick your battles! Not every small infraction should incur your wrath. Pay attention to the big picture and things that will affect their life. Address those issues, and let the small stuff slide.

Let your child make their own decisions. Do not give them dozens of options, but do give them two and let them decide. Blue jeans or khaki pants? Macaroni and cheese for lunch, or a peanut butter and honey sandwich? Tapering down the choices so they do not have to concentrate on many things at the same time, you are helping them learn to make choices without overwhelming them.

Always remember that your child's ADHD does not reflect on your parenting skills. Some people insist that ADHD does not exist, and we know that simply is not the case. ADHD is a medical condition, and no one is to blame.

Children with ADHD are constantly on the go, and they are very demanding, and sometimes uncooperative. It is not your fault, it is just the way they are. As a parent, the way your child behaves can make you proud or ashamed; many parents of ADHD kids feel guilty because their children act the way they do.

There is no right or wrong way to be a parent. You have to do what works for your family and your child. Remember, as hard as it is to deal with your child, that child is dealing with a lot of issues as well, and looking to you for the love and guidance they need.

There must be more people involved in raising a child with ADHD than just the parent. Entire families and even extended families can help and become active in the treatment of a child with the disorder.

Here's a testimonial from a happy parent:

> *"When my son Fraser first came to see Enza, he found it hard to concentrate at school and was very disruptive in class, at home we found it hard doing homework with him and also telling him to do chores.*
>
> *After the first few sessions with Enza, we noticed changes in him. He became calmer and also happier in himself. Fraser's last school report was great. It was amazing to see the changes he had made not only in his behaviour yet also grades and concentration. His friend's parents have also noticed Fraser being calmer and not hyperactive like he once was.*
>
> *Now Fraser is up to his ninth session and looking back we have noticed that Fraser isn't as emotional as he used to be. He is calmer and happier with himself. School grades have improved. He has got 4 As and 3 Bs in his last report. He is at the same class level and isn't being a distraction to the rest of the class. Fraser has improved a lot and we always notice an improvement after doing Brain Gym®. As parents of a child that needed help in schooling, behavioural and social difficulties, we would highly recommend Enza's services using Brain Gym® and Rhythmic Movement. It has really helped our son and our family. To see our son happy and content with himself is the ultimate reward."*   Tanya, Mother

CHAPTER 10

Your child's self-esteem

It is critical that your child has adequate self-esteem. Self-esteem does not mean that we are braggarts or egotistical, it means that we value ourselves and our personal achievements, and have a positive sense of self-worth.

Self-esteem in children is vital because it helps children to be proud of themselves and gives them power to believe they can do and try new things, while helping them to develop respect for themselves. That self-respect also leads to earning the respect of other people.

A child's self-esteem is shaped by a number of things:

- How he or she thinks

- What he or she expects of himself or herself

- How other people react and interact with him or her

- How other people (family, friends, and teachers) think and feel about him or her

Many, but not all, children with ADHD have difficulties with school, with teachers, and sometimes with their families. These children often find it difficult to make and keep friends as well. Often, people do not understand their behaviour and judge them harshly because of it. They can be very disruptive, and are often ostracized for their behaviour, so at times they tend not to bother trying to fit in.

All these things can cause children with ADHD to feel poorly about themselves. They may believe they are stupid, bad, or losers. It is no wonder that their self-esteem is low and they find it difficult to think or say anything that is positive or good about themselves.

Disruptive behaviour is one of the key characteristics of ADHD, and children with the disorder cannot help their behaviour. Well-meaning teachers attempting to cope with an entire classroom full of children sometimes deal with ADHD by excluding the child from the class.

Happy events for other children, like birthday parties and other social events, can become sources of pain for those children with ADHD. Other parents will often exclude "problem" children from their party lists, effectively shutting out the child with ADHD and reinforcing their negative feelings of self-worth.

How can you build your child's self-esteem?

To combat all of the negative things that occur, it is necessary for you to help your child's self-esteem in a number of ways.

> **Praise:** Helping your child feel positive is vital, and praising him or her as often as possible helps tremendously. Verbal praise on a regular basis is important, and a small physical reward for special accomplishments is better still.

> **Love:** This should go without saying, but your unconditional

love is absolutely the best gift you can give your child. Do not tell your child they are bad; tell your child that their behaviour is bad. No matter how they behave, the child needs to understand you are always there for them.

➤ **Trust:** Be sure that your child knows you will always "have them back" no matter what happens. You and your child are a team, and you work together towards common goals. Be sure they know how special they are to you and that you trust and respect them.

➤ **Goals:** Together, set goals for your child that can be achieved easily, and watch as your child gains self-confidence before your eyes.

➤ **Sports and hobbies:** Having a hobby or being a part of a club can build self-esteem. Allow your child to decide what sort of hobbies or activities they want to be part of—do not push them in a direction that appeals to you. No matter what the hobby—dancing, baseball, swimming, karate, cooking, or crafts—your child will learn new things and be proud of them. Be prepared for them to suddenly lose interest in one activity and move on to something else; that is fairly common with ADHD kids.

➤ **Positive focus:** Always focus on positive things. Have your child make a list of what she likes about herself—positive attributes and cool things she can do. Post it on the wall in her room on the refrigerator where she will see it often and can add to it regularly. Likewise, if she has a bad day at school, have her make a list of things she is grateful for, so that she realizes that even when something bad happens, there is so much good in the world, and in people.

People who hear a lot of criticism often have low self-esteem, whether the criticism is very accurate or not. Teaching your child the proper ways to deal with criticism are very important. Here are some tips on how a child can handle criticism:

- Have them listen to what is being said without interrupting or making excuses. In fact, teach them to agree with points that are possibly correct.

- Next have them ask questions if something seems unclear.

- Have them admit mistakes and apologize when it is warranted.

- If the criticism is unfair or untrue, teach them to politely say, "I do not agree with that." This is a good alternative to being resentful and angry then hitting the other child.

Obviously, some people are better than others at accepting criticism, and certainly it is a part of life that they will need to be aware of and know how to handle without an emotional meltdown.

On the other hand, if you are sarcastic or overly negative toward your ADHD child, this criticism can undermine all of the positive things you do for her. However, to help teach your child how to accept criticism, it is important for you to offer it in a constructive way. Be calm, only expressing anger appropriately without upsetting the other person and focus on the behaviour you want to change. Never criticize the person, just the behaviour. Find some positive things to say to balance out the criticism as well, and start and end on upbeat notes. When forming your sentences, use "I" instead of "you' as it sounds less accusatory and aggressive.

If your child is struggling with their school work, NEVER say "You're stupid!" Instead, tell him that you were so impressed how he understood those fraction problems, and that if he re-reads the instructions, you know he will better understand these ones about currency. Focus on the positives, and ignore the negatives. You will both be better off for it.

Be sure that your child understands how to give criticism nicely as well. Have them tell their friend that "I like playing outside with you, but I have to finish my homework first. Maybe we can play this weekend." This is much better than bluntly saying, "No, I'm not coming out."

Overall, it is important for him or her to learn the coping mechanisms to deal with criticism without it adversely affecting their self-esteem, and to teach them to communicate well with their peers, family, and teachers.

In 1982, a study by Jack Canfield, an expert on self esteem, involved 100 children. They were to keep track for a day about the positive and negative comments given to them; on average, each child received 460 negative comments or critical comments and only 75 positive or supportive comments. That is over six times more negative than positive. So, it is vital throughout the growing process that children receive tons of positive encouragement.

Another thing I have always believed is that a critical element of developing healthy self-esteem is being able to look beyond yourself and to the needs of others. Doing something genuinely nice for someone else always makes you feel good, as well as helps the other person. I think it is important to teach our children to do that regularly. That means thinking about how someone else may be feeling or what they may be going through. Being respectful to other people and their belongings. To look beyond themselves, to others and the world around them.

Here's another happy parent. This is what she says:

"Our 8 year old son Morgan struggled with his reading, spelling, concentration and confidence. He was always worrying about what he thought he didn't know and should. He also had trouble getting to sleep most nights.

After his first few sessions with Enza, we noticed an improvement in Morgan's school work and self-confidence. From there we kept noticing changes with each session. Now it's hard to believe he's the same child. He is now a very happy confident boy, achieving great results at school, willing to speak up about different subjects and feeling and knowing he is as important as all of us in the world."
Janet, Mother

CHAPTER 11

Turning bad behaviour into cooperation

Every child misbehaves on occasion, and even the best children sometimes can be aggressive. It is more common for children with ADHD to have behaviour problems; the core symptoms of the disorder—impulsiveness, inattention, distractibility, and hyperactivity, each affects the way your child is able to interact with others. It is especially important to note that your child interacts the way she can, not necessarily the way she wants.

Take a look at these symptoms and how they can affect a child, for a better understanding of your child.

Hyperactivity causes fidgeting, excessive talking, and inability to play quietly. This part of the disorder can cause the child to break things – their own and others' – and causes them to play roughly with other kids.

Impulsivity makes it hard for the child not to blurt out answers or interrupt others' conversations. The child might speak without considering how and what they say could hurt someone or lash out because the child is frustrated.

Inattention causes the child problems following directions, and they might appear to have not listened at all. That usually is not the case; the child may have tried to understand but just could not focus.

While we know these behaviours can drive us to distraction, we need to constantly remind ourselves that the child is not intentionally doing any of these things. It is all part of the disorder. Of course, these children receive plenty of critical comments and negativity from others.

In fact, negative relating and parenting styles are believed to greatly increase the probability of aggressive and anti-social behaviour. If it is left unchecked, it often leads to more serious problems, like oppositional or conduct disorder.

Luckily, there is an easy three part process that will help with behavioural problems.

1. Encourage positive behaviour. You can do this by using attention, praise, and rewards for special times.

2. Reduce negative behaviour. You will do this by setting clear and consistent rules, and enforced consequences for breaking the rules.

3. Brain Gym® exercises. Performing these exercises on a daily basis will improve your child's behaviour, learning ability, and listening and reasoning skills.

Children with ADHD thrive, and their behaviour is much better, when there is structure, consistency in their lives and an exercise movement program like Brain Gym. Always stick with a routine that they are used to every day.

Working with your child

It is important to allow your child some input into the rule-making process. Decide on the rules together; sit down and get out pencil and paper and negotiate these things with your child. Maybe they want to stay up a little later, but they are willing to get themselves ready for bed without any nagging. That is a good tradeoff, isn't it? It sure beats following them around making sure they brushed their teeth and have laid out their clothes.

When you feel strongly about something, make sure your child knows that, and the reason why you feel that way. For instance, putting all of their books and papers into their backpack when finished with them means there will be no mad hunt for them in the morning.

Some very effective ways to reduce bad behaviour are also relatively easy:

> ➤ Address your child by name and speak clearly to ensure you have his attention.

> ➤ Make your commands or instructions short and simple. (Bite-sized pieces.)

> ➤ Punishments need to be quick and easily enforceable.

> ➤ Brain Gym® exercises done with your child help them calm down, focus, and improve attention.

It's not always possible to ignore them when they do something bad; you should have some pre-determined negative consequences for times when they break a rule. These instant, mild punishments can go a long way toward reducing bad behaviour. Consequences that cost your child something they value—time, money, or taking away something that is important to them - helps to decrease aggressiveness and other poor behaviour.

Why do punishments fail?

Many parents implement punishments and then do not understand why it did not work. Of course, we have all seen "silly" punishments at work as well—consider the teenager's parents who ground her three months for coming home late, and then she talks her way out of the house in three days.

Punishments fail for the following reasons

1. It is too severe (three months is a little excessive)

2. It is inconsistent (Mom and Dad obviously were not on the same page when one of them allowed her out of the house in a few days.)

3. It is administered too late.

At times, natural consequences can be enough. Toss your drink on the floor, and you will become thirsty.

Time-outs helps when it is a temper tantrum that you are dealing with, the idea being that they will calm down in a few minutes and can rejoin the family. Sitting in a corner or the bottom of a set of steps is a good place for a time-out. With small children, five minutes is plenty; raise it to ten or fifteen minutes for older kids.

Taking away privileges like TV, computer, or video games help discourage bad behaviour. So does taking away their allowance. Do make the punishments reasonable, though, and impose them for just a day so that they can start tomorrow with a clean slate. Be careful not to do this too often as resentment and anger can build up towards you and you lose the purpose of discouraging the bad behaviour. Find out what is causing the bad behaviour to resolve it properly.

Never give out punishment that will hurt your child physically or emotionally. Never insult your child in public, and never get violent with them.

Be careful that you never appear to be rewarding bad behaviour—we have all seen the child throwing a temper tantrum in the store, until the parent gives in and buys what the child has been demanding. What did that child just learn? They learned an effective way to manipulate their parents.

Always be consistent and keep consequences small and immediate. The consistency is what makes the punishment effective. You should, however, monitor the effect of the punishment, and when it loses its effectiveness, it is time to change strategies.

After an episode, when your child is calm, talk to him or her and clearly state what you want changed and why their behaviour was wrong. Do not ask them "why" they did something—tantrums and other episodes are typically the way ADHD children express what they cannot tell you in words. Asking why will lead to more frustration for both of you. Watch your child for the next couple of days, and if she has listened to what you said, tell her how pleased you are with her.

If punishments you have decided on do not seem to faze your child, try something else. Think of things they really like, and then let them know those things will be taken away—whether that is a karate class or their cell phone. You might sometimes find that a punishment which works well one day does not matter to them on another, so you might need to constantly change things to keep up with your child's energy.

CHAPTER 12

How to improve learning for school success?

Having a school-aged ADHD child can be one of life's most difficult situations. ADHD children need lots of attention and constant supervision to be kept on task, which can be difficult for a teacher with a classroom full of children to handle.

ADHD students can be amazingly disorganised, with their desks stuffed with supplies and papers. They cannot sit still unless they are totally engrossed in the lesson you are teaching, and they frequently interrupt. At times it takes extreme patience to deal with an ADHD child in a classroom setting. The flipside is that these children can be an absolute joy as well—great workers, funny, and very personable and loving.

Structure overall is a great thing for ADHD children—but the classroom setting is challenging because it requires sitting quietly and focusing. It is often difficult keeping ADHD children on task and making sure they do not fall behind in their studies. Some start out strong and then seem to get a little further behind every week. They lose homework papers that they have spent hours on, or study intently for a test and still do not do well—sometimes making them want to give up in frustration.

ADHD is often recognized in the third grade, and the students are referred for treatment. They are expected to do a lot more work independently, and this is what allows the teacher to tell which children are capable of independent work and which are not. More referrals are seen in seventh grade, as the child leaves elementary school for middle school, with many different classes and different teachers.

Here are some things you, and your child's teacher, can do to help your child be successful in school:

> ➢ Make sure the classroom rules are clear and they understand them, and that they are posted in the classroom or on their desk.

> ➢ Find your ADHD child a seat close to the teacher, and away from as many distractions as possible.

> ➢ Enlist your child's teacher to assist—have him or her help keep a journal of your child's daily behaviour. Provide immediate feedback when there is a problem, or when they have an especially great day.

> ➢ Utilize positive praise and rewards when the child behaves well all day, or all week.

> ➢ Recess! Be sure that the child gets a break to be able to get up and walk around, even if that is just to the water fountain or to drop something off at the office for the teacher.

> ➢ Break tasks down into smaller chunks, to help the student stay on task. If his history assignment is to read two chapters—have him do one, take a short break and then come back to finish.

> ➢ Use concise directions—do not overload him with information.

➤ Put a hand on the child's shoulder to help him focus when talking to him.

➤ Let the student have a stress ball or some silly putty to manipulate; even the slightest stimulation can sometimes keep him focused.

➤ Be sure his most difficult subjects are scheduled for morning when he is fresh.

➤ Pair the ADHD student with a "study buddy"—one of the kind and mature kids that can help keep him on track.

Be aware that school will likely be a struggle for your ADHD child, and do all you can to help him. Get him plenty of physical activity and allow him to study in short bursts rather than marathon sessions. Encourage him with lots of positive praise with completed tasks, and treat him to something good if his report card shows how hard he is trying.

As an educator, what can you do to help your ADHD child in the classroom?

Here is how a teacher used Brain Gym® in an unruly classroom:

"I find the younger children respond well to Brain Gym®.

Brain Gym® helps me to calm down and have a more peaceful disposition. This in turn helps me to relate to the students more effectively.

Just recently in a class of grade 4 students, a couple of girls were fighting. Both dissolved in tears and wouldn't work. It was disruptive to the rest of the class to have them whinging. I stopped the lesson, did the Brain Gym® exercise - Hookups with the class, and the hysterics stopped. I was relief teacher at the time. When the

---

class teacher came back everyone was settled and quiet.

I found letter and number reversals by students easy to correct by getting them to do the exercises lazy eights, elephant ears and double doodles. I also write the numbers and letters on their backs while they draw what they feel me doing. If more teachers saw Brain Gym® as being a tool for more productive teaching, and actually making better use of class time, they would not be saying they have no time to do it.

After an hour of working when students are restless, a drink of water and Brain Gym® refreshes everyone - including me - to keep on going."

Sandra Petersen, teacher

Carla Hannaford, neurophysiologist and educator, comments from her book, *"Smart Moves"*

"This experience greatly reinforced my conviction that movement was somehow essential to learning. My growing realization that the body was just as important as the brain when it came to learning led to the questioning and study which resulted in this book....We have spent years and resources struggling to teach people to learn, and yet the standardized achievement test scores go down and illiteracy rises. Could it be that one of the key elements we've been missing is simply movement?... It's time to take a serious look at our own misconceptions about our bodies. In so doing we can free the mind/body system to reclaim its infinite potential for learning, thought and creativity."

Introducing Brain Gym® to increase grades

Brain Gym® is a fun learning program that assists in all stages of childhood development, language development, coordination, gross motor skills and fine motor skills, stress relief, creativity and problem solving. Children love Brain Gym® because it puts them in charge of their success.

Here's how to unlock your child's immense potential and help them be calm, focused and confident in school and in life. It's a simple, drug-free learning program that takes only 15 minutes per day and they'll have fun doing it! Your child can make positive changes.

Brain Gym® is the result of over 30 years of development by Paul E. Dennison, PhD and Gail E. Dennison, pioneers in applied brain research. It is now taught in more than 80 countries within schools, corporations, performing arts programs and sports centres. The success of these techniques has been proven in clinical experience, field studies and published reports. Now, the latest scientific research shows us how it works.

The discovery of neuroplasticity, hailed as one of the most important scientific breakthroughs of the 20th century, has proven that the brain can rewire itself throughout our lives in response to thinking, learning and movement. In fact, all learning, from the time we are babies, involves movement. As we grow, we move and learn and the brain forms new nerve cells and neural connections – the superhighways for intellectual and physical performance.

When you use Brain Gym® in your classroom:

> ➤ You and your students are more relaxed and ready to work together for the whole day

➢ You and your students feel mentally 'switched on' and energized

➢ Communication and group interaction becomes more positive and productive

➢ Students are able to concentrate, listen, are motivated and retain information

➢ Students become motivated, achieve better grades and become more desirous of more learning and success.

As a parent, what can you do to help your ADHD child for school success

Brain Gym® uses simple exercises and techniques to enhance and integrate the left and right hemispheres of the brain for amazing, often immediate, results. Brain Gym® increases brain fitness for adults and children:

➢ The exercises are fun, easy and take only 15 minutes per day

➢ They get better grades, perform better in sports and the arts, and relate better to friends and family

➢ They can work through whatever anxieties or fears are holding them back

➢ They can feel the difference almost immediately and this gives them confidence

➢ They learn techniques to help them overcome any problem or difficult situation.

The Brain Gym® workshop has been a great help to my students and my own daughter

"I use Brain Gym® with my students and it greatly improves their concentration and ability to focus on their lessons. On a personal level, the greatest success I've had is with my own daughter. A reluctant reader and a quiet student, Brain Gym® has been instrumental in greatly increasing her self-confidence. She has improved in all academic areas and is a happier child. I strongly recommend Brain Gym to all. Thank you for providing us with the power to succeed." Joanne, Teacher, Mother

The twenty-six enjoyable Brain Gym® activities support the development of key sensorimotor abilities – readiness skills – that make learning easier and more pleasurable. These activities are uniquely designed to fulfill specific physical requirements that learners encounter in the classroom. While any physical education may 'wake up' the brain, the twenty-six Brain Gym® activities further foster the flexibility, eye teaming and hand-eye coordination that allow learners to thrive in the classroom, along with the ability to live happily and creatively amid the stressors of modern life.

The use of these activities throughout the day can relieve stress. It can be a quick mind body warm up before studying, writing, sports or music playing, bringing them to feel relaxed, alert and productive.

As a parent, Brain Gym® can help you too!

Not only will you experience the joy of watching your child become happier, healthier, more relaxed and more confident, you can also learn to use Brain Gym® to improve your own physical, mental and emotional well-being. Brain Gym® is a safe, natural physical therapy that can help the whole family with stress relief, workplace performance, health problems, anxiety, depression and relationships.

Find out more about Brain Gym® and how to easily implement it into your daily routine and make a huge difference for you and your child. You can learn these simple yet powerful techniques through one-on-one sessions and workshops. You can make contact with a licensed Brain Gym® instructor in your area.

Experience the benefits of one-on-one sessions and attend Brain Gym® workshops to learn how to implement the Brain Gym® effectively into your life. The programs will help you and your family bring harmony, good health and success as it has done for many children and adults. I fully recommend hands on training in learning how to use the Brain Gym® program through one-on-one sessions or workshops in your area. You will personally benefit from the program as I did when I first attended in 1986.

Workshops for schools

Teacher in-services: Gives classroom teachers the knowledge and practice needed to use Brain Gym® in the classroom. Teachers learn to master some of the Brain Gym® movements and learn when, where and why to use the movements with their students. Full day format is perfect for teacher professional development days.

Find out how Brain Gym® can help you and your students create a calmer, happier and more productive classroom. The Brain Gym® program offers a learning system that utilizes only hands, heart and movement without undue dependence on materials, equipment or technology.

There are many books and resources available on the subject. I have placed a list of some of the books I recommend at the back of the book. On the website www.dlhc.com.au I have a recommended a huge selection at Enza's Store.

Imagine your students ...

- relaxed and able to concentrate in school

- confident that they can do their best in any situation – whether learning, creating or playing sport

- happy, relating well to others, and not overwhelmed by negative emotions

- empowered to follow their own path to personal success and fulfilment.

Whether you're a parent or an educator, there is support out there to achieve success in the classroom and in whatever tasks you pursue in life using these simple techniques and exercises.

I highly recommend parents and teachers to attend Brain Gym® Workshops to have hands on practical training. They will experience the benefits for themselves. In so doing, parents will be able to assist their children at home and teachers assist their students in the classroom successfully. Allowing an experienced Brain Gym® consultant design an individualized program will assist your child resolve learning difficulties faster and easily.

CHAPTER 13

Conclusion

Poor concentration, reading difficulties, forgetfulness, anxiety, uncontrollable emotional outbursts, inability to relate to others – these are all roadblocks that undermine a child's capacity to develop to their full potential. When these symptoms are formally diagnosed as a learning or attention disorder such as ADD or ADHD, it can be very demoralizing for the child and also negatively impact on the family as a whole – increasing stress and disharmony within the home.

For those children and adults diagnosed with ADD or ADHD, and their families, it is important to have access to a range of information so that the most appropriate treatment strategy is chosen. In traditional medicine, drugs are often the first choice. But, given the potentially detrimental short and long term effects of these drugs, it is not surprising that many people are now seeking alternative natural and behavioural therapies.

The precise causes of ADHD may not be known, but it is clear that brain development and function is a key factor. It seems obvious to first employ safe, educational movement programs, such as Brain Gym® and Rhythmic Movement Training. The Brain Gym® movements have been shown in field studies, published research, and clinical experience to prepare children with the physical skills they need in order to learn to read, write, and otherwise function effectively in the classroom and in their lives. The ability to learn easily is especially important for children in the first years of life and school, when they are laying the foundation for achieving higher-level developmental milestones for play, school, work, and daily living. This can only be beneficial for general health and well-being, and may reduce or eliminate the need for medication.

Brain Gym® and Rhythmic Movement Training are drug-free solutions that use simple movements and techniques to improve brain development and balanced brain function. These fun exercises take only 15 minutes a day and produce results almost immediately.

In my practice as a licensed Brain Gym® consultant/teacher and Rhythmic Movement Trainer, I have personally witnessed the extraordinary transformation of children struggling with early learning difficulties such as ADD or ADHD as they:

➢ dissolve the physical, emotional and mental obstacles holding them back from their full potential

➢ gain calm confidence and replace negative thoughts such as, "I can't do this," or, "I'm not good enough," with new positive patterns of self-affirmation

➢ are empowered to access and use their innate learning, reasoning and creative capabilities

➢ 'switch-on' for better communication, relate more easily with others and feel happier at school and at home

➢ take charge of their own success to achieve higher grades and perform better in sports and music.

Brain Gym® and Rhythmic Movement Training is not just for those with diagnosed ADD or ADHD, it can also help the whole family with stress relief, workplace performance, health problems, anxiety, depression and relationships.

More information is available through my website at www.dlhc.com.au.

There is a list of further ADD, ADHD and Brain Gym® and Rhythmic Movement Training resources at the end of this book.

I trust you have found this information helpful in making decisions about the well-being of your family, and invite you to email me with any questions you may have.

I wish you and your family vibrant health, mental clarity and radiant well-being.

Enza Lyons
Licensed Brain Gym® Teacher /Consultant (Brain Gym® International)
Learning & Behaviour Specialist
Rhythmic Movement Training Consultant
Workplace Performance Coach
Brisbane, Australia
https://calendly.com/enzalyons
Phone: 0413 697 692

CHAPTER 14

Finding support

ADHD is one of the most pressing problems for both adults and children in our world today. With all of our technological advances, children are not getting the physical exercise and stimulation that they require for normal development. ADHD was virtually unheard of twenty or thirty years ago, but now it is commonplace and most people know an adult or a child that has been diagnosed and is being medicated. ADHD, and the psychotropic drugs used to combat it, in particular are highly controversial.

Many healthcare practitioners and parents feel that our kids are over-medicated. Others believe that labeling children with this tag is not helpful to them, and may cause them more harm than good. Still others feel it is simply a cop-out for parents to explain their children's poor behaviour.

The bottom line is people act the way they do for a reason. If behaviours are beyond their control, a medical exam could be done and possibilities explored.

Adults with ADHD face additional problems; they likely have been afflicted for many years, and since there is now a name for the disorder, they might feel some relief about the way they feel, and their behaviour. Finding methods to cope with those behaviours can make their life easier.

Having a normal life is possible—even though a person has ADHD. You need to face it head on, deal with the issues, learn to live with it, and ultimately conquer it. Get ready for a world that works for you!

So where do you find that support?

Books and resources

There are many books and resources relating to learning, child development and the Brain Gym® program. My recommendations can be found on my website at www.dlhc.com.au at Enza's Store.

Smart Moves: Why Learning Is Not All In Your Head. Carla Hannaford. Salt Lake City: Great River Books, 2005

Awakening the Child Heart. Handbook of Global Parenting. Carla Hannaford. Captain Cook: Jamilla Nur, 2002

Brain Gym®: Teachers Edition: The Companion Guide to Brain Gym®: Simple Activities for Whole-Brain Learning. Paul E. Dennison Ph.D and Gail E. Dennison. Ventura: Edu-Kinesthetics, 2010

Brain Gym® and Me: Reclaiming the Pleasure of Learning. Paul E. Dennison Ph.D and Gail E. Dennison. Ventura: Edu-Kinesthetics, 2006

Brain Gym®: Simple Activities for Whole Brain Learning. Paul E. Dennison and Gail E. Dennison. Ventura: Edu-Kinesthetics, 2000

Movements that Heal: Rhythmic Movement Training and Primitive Reflexes Integration: a drug-free approach to learning, emotional and behavioural challenges. Harald Blomberg M.D. with Moira Dempsey, 2011

Educate Your Brain: Use Mind-Body Balance To Learn Faster, Work Smarter and Move More Easily Through Life. Kathy Brown. Balance Point Publishing, 2012

Reflexes, Learning and Behaviour: A Window into the Child's Mind. Sally Goddard. Eugene: Fern Ridge Press, 2002

The Brain That Changes Itself: Stories of Personal Triumph from the Frontiers of Brain Science. Norman Doidge. New York: Penguin, 2007

Hands On: How to Use Brain Gym® in the Classroom. Isabel Cohen and Marcelle Goldsmith. Ventura: Edu-Kinesthetics, 2000

CD/Book: *Movement & Learning: The Children's Song Book and Music CD.* Brendan O'Hara. Victoria, Australia: The F# Music Company, 1991

Is Your Child's Brain Starving? Dr. Michael R. Lyon MD & Dr. G. Christine Laurell Ph.D

Water: For Health, For Healing, For Life: You're Not Sick, You're Thirsty. Dr. F. Batmanghelidj. M.D. New York: Riverhead, 2006

Brain Gym® and Edu-K courses

Brain Gym® International/Educational Kinesiology Foundation –

To find worldwide Brain Gym® teachers and consultants –

www.braingym.org   Around the World

www.braingym.org.au   Australia

https://calendly.com/enzalyons Enza Lyons, Brisbane, Qld, Australia

Phone: 0413 697 692

RMT Classes worldwide, teachers and consultants

www.rhythmicmovement.com

Contact Enza Lyons for more information on Personal Consultations, Workshops, Bookstore and Online Learning.

Brain Gym® is a registered trademark of Brain Gym® International/Educational Kinesiology Foundation.

Enza Lyons, shares her insights as a Parent, Grandparent, Learning & Behaviour s Specialist in child development, Licensed Brain Gym Consultant and Instructor, Support teacher and Kinesiologist. She has been involved with Brain Gym since 1986. For over 30 years in her private practice, she has assisted children and adults struggling with concentration, memory, comprehension, reading, writing, math, anxiety, depression, trauma, pain, early learning difficulties such as ADHD, dyspraxia, dyslexia, autism and delayed development. Clearly one can see these children are intelligent, just stuck.

Many children and adults have transformed their lives with outstanding results using effective and nonconventional educational learning programs as shown in the book. Enza is the creator of Calm Happy Confident Child System. This program can unlock your child's hidden talents to learn, create, move and achieve more success at school and in life.

Young parents can be better informed to assist them in making better choices to help their children build confidence, self-esteem, increase their ability to learn and relate better to others. Enza shares her passion and enthusiasm with others through courses, workshops, in-house school training, live zoom classes and consultations, conference presentations and her personal one on one sessions.

Are you doing things the hard way through trial and error or would you like to learn the easy faster way to get results? Contact Enza for more information on how to help you get faster results with a proven effective system and framework within 30 days.

www.ingramcontent.com/pod-product-compliance
Lightning Source LLC
Chambersburg PA
CBHW072151020426
42334CB00018B/1951